Observing, Assessing and Planning for Children in the Early Years

How can your observations of young children be properly used and understood?

This introductory text shows how, by observing children knowledgeably, early years practitioners can plan for and assess the young children in their care much more effectively.

Each chapter contains practical advice, case studies, summaries and a glossary of key terms, making this book a perfect, highly accessible introduction to:

▶ the work of key people who have become famous for their skills as observers;
▶ the theories behind their work and how this can be related to the day-to-day nursery environment;
▶ observation, assessment and the planning cycle in relation to the Foundation Stage Curriculum.

Early years practitioners and students should find this a helpful and readable guide to improving their practice. It will also be invaluable to students studying childcare and early years education.

Sandra Smidt was Director of Undergraduate Programmes in the School of Education and Community Studies, University of East London. She is currently working as an education consultant.

The Nursery World/Routledge Essential Guides for Early Years Practitioners

Books in this series address key issues for early years practitioners working in today's nursery and school environments. Each title is packed full of practical activities, support, advice and guidance, all of which is in line with current government early years policy. The authors use their experience and expertise to write accessibly and informatively, emphasising through the use of case studies the practical aspects of the subject, whilst retaining strong theoretical underpinnings throughout.

These titles will encourage the practitioner and student alike to gain greater confidence and authority in their day-to-day work, offering many illustrative examples of good practice, suggestions for further reading and many invaluable resources. For a handy, clear and inspirational guide to understanding the important and practical issues, the early years practitioner or student need look no further then this series.

Titles in the series:

Circle Time for Young Children
Jenny Mosley

Helping with Behaviour
Sue Roffey

Identifying Additional Learning Needs: listening to the children
Christine Macintyre

Observing, Assessing and Planning for Children in the Early Years
Sandra Smidt

Encouraging Creative Play and Learning (forthcoming)
Diane Rich

Observing, Assessing and Planning for Children in the Early Years

Sandra Smidt

 Routledge
Taylor & Francis Group
LONDON AND NEW YORK

NURSERY
WORLD

First published 2005
by Routledge
2 Park Square, Milton Park, Abingdon, Oxon OX14 4RN

Simultaneously published in the USA and Canada
by Routledge
270 Madison Ave, New York, NY 10016

Routledge is an imprint of the Taylor & Francis Group

© 2005 Sandra Smidt

Typeset in Perpetua and Bell Gothic by
Florence Production Ltd, Stoodleigh, Devon
Printed and bound in Great Britain by
TJ International Ltd, Padstow, Cornwall

Key Guides for Effective Teaching in Higher Education web resource

The Key Guides for Effective Teaching in Higher Education Series provides
guidance and advice for those looking to improve their teaching and learning.
It is accompanied by a useful website which features brand new supplementary
material, including How Students Learn, a guide written by Professor George
Brown which provides outlines and commentaries on theories of learning and
their implications for teaching practice.

Visit the website at: http://www.routledgefalmer.com/series/KGETHE

The Routledge website also features a wide range of books for lecturers and
higher education professionals

British Library Cataloguing in Publication Data
A catalogue record for this book is available from the British Library

Library of Congress Cataloging in Publication Data
A catalog record for this book has been requested

ISBN 0–415–33973–1 (hbk)
ISBN 0–415–33974–X (pbk)

Contents

For Hannah, Ben, Chloe,
Jake and Zac in recognition
of all the significant moments
they have offered.

Introduction

The place of observation in early years education

This book is about observation and its role in early years education. Observation – watching what others do and listening to what they say – is something we all do all the time in classrooms and out of them. We sit in cafés or in parks and watch the other people going by. We listen to conversations going on around us on the bus or train. But the observation that we are talking about in this book is different in that we do it for a purpose.

Observation is the best tool we have for understanding if and how children are learning. Put at its simplest, if we observe Johnny on Monday and he can build a tower of two blocks we know that that is something he can already do. If we observe him on Tuesday and see him build a tower of four blocks we know that he has developed his motor skills so that they have become sufficiently refined for him to build a four-block tower. In other words, we have evidence that he has made progress. That is a very crude example but illustrates the purpose of observation we are concerned with in this book.

If you are already working in a school or another educational setting you will already be involved in observing children and may well have been on courses about observation. It is an essential part of most training courses for teaching assistants, nursery nurses and teachers, and there are many school and LEA-based training days focusing on observation and assessment. So you may well be familiar with many aspects of observation, and the purpose of this book is to provide you with something you can keep and refer to as you embed observation as an assessment tool in your daily practice. You will know that in order to use observation as an assessment tool each observation you make needs to be considered in light of what you know about how children learn. You can read more about this in Chapter 3.

Those working in reception classes have a familiarity with observation – how, when, where and why – through having to implement the Foundation Stage Profile. This is the assessment required to be made for children in reception classes so that they can be given a 'baseline level' as they move from the Foundation Stage to Key Stage 1. The Profile parallels the Standard Assessment Tasks (SATS) which take place at the end of all the Key Stages; it is different in that it is based on observation rather than on testing. Some people believe that the demands (in terms of time) of the Profile are excessive and there are currently fierce debates surrounding its future. Indeed Professor Ted Wragg wrote scathingly about it in an article in the *Guardian* in March 2003. He described the Profile as 'a horrendous labelling scheme [that] required reception class teachers to grade five-year-olds by putting somewhere between 3,000 and 10,000 ticks and crosses in boxes'.

Wragg went on to say that although experts and trainers were describing the Profile as requiring formative and summative assessment (and you will learn more about those terms in Chapter 2), for him it is nothing more than ticking boxes. Many others agree with Wragg and the debate continues to roll on. Some educationalists fiercely defend the Profile, perhaps because they see it as the only possible alternative to testing.

One of the things that all educationalists need to consider is how to build observation and assessment into their daily programme. Of course, everyone observes children casually at all times of the day and in most activities. What observation as an assessment tool requires is a system for ensuring that all adults have time to observe individual children or children in small groups, focusing on aspects of learning and being able to record what they see and hear. You will easily be able to recognise how impossible it would be for you to record what you see and hear for each child in each activity every day of the year. It is essential that the team of workers (teacher, nursery nurse, teaching assistant, support teachers) works out a plan for each week, deciding who will watch which children and in what activities and for what purposes. You will be able to read more about this in Chapter 3.

The book is set out like this:

▷ In Chapter 1 you are introduced to the work of some educational experts who have used observation as a tool, and you are then invited to learn more about how observation helps us know more about all the children we work with. This means thinking about each child as an individual with a history, a language, a culture and a family – all of which are significant in learning and development.

▷ In Chapter 2 we define assessment, and talk about the different types of assessment and the purposes of each. We also examine the differences between assessment and testing.

▷ Chapter 3 is, in a sense, the key chapter in this book. It talks about what we know about how children learn, since knowing how children learn is essential to understanding and interpreting what we observe. It also starts looking at how to introduce workable systems for assessment.

▷ Chapter 4 is devoted to using observations to help children take the next step in learning. It is about giving feedback and marking work.

▷ Chapter 5 gives you the opportunity to practise your skills of analysing observations, using what you have learned about children's learning. It is made up of a series of observations and case studies.

▷ Chapter 6 talks about all the people who can and should be involved in assessing children's progress – teachers, nursery nurses, teaching assistants, children themselves, their parents and experts (speech therapists, educational psychologists, etc.).

▷ Chapter 7 takes the arguments about having a system for tracking progress further by considering how to keep records, use profiles and have conferences with both children and parents.

▷ Chapter 8 is the final chapter of the book and looks at the statutory requirements in terms of reporting to parents and in terms of accountability.

Chapter 1

The thinking observer

✔ In this chapter you will be introduced to observation as a tool for learning more about children.

✔ You will read some famous examples of observations and see how they have enabled the authors to understand more about individual children.

✔ You will consider the concept of 'the thinking observer' and see if it makes sense to you.

✔ You will think about how observation can help you know more about children whose cultures, languages and experiences might not be familiar to you.

✔ You will be introduced to the idea that observation itself is a learning tool and something that is used by both children and adults.

In 1964 a famous play therapist called Virginia Axline wrote a book called *Dibs: In Search of Self*. Axline traced the progress of a 5-year-old boy called Dibs and described by his school as a 'defective'. Through her observations of Dibs at play Axline began to understand his fears, his dreams and his abilities. People who have read the book have often found it intensely moving, as illustrated by this brief passage where Dibs buries three toy soldiers in the sand:

'This makes them unhappy', he said. 'They cannot see. They cannot hear. They cannot breathe', he explained. 'Dibs, dig them out of there', he ordered himself. 'First thing you know it'll be time to go. Do you want to leave them buried, Dibs?' he asked himself.

(Axline 1964: 67)

Later, in the same observation, he identifies one of the soldiers as 'Papa' and proceeds to knock him down time and time again. You may want to speculate on why he does this and what it means for him: you may want to read the book for yourself. What is clear is that the observer – Axline – is able to build up a picture of Dibs, which she is then able to use to help her 'treat' him.

Those of us working with young children are not primarily concerned with treating children but rather with understanding what they can do, what they are interested in and what they already know.

We can go further back in time to the work of Susan Isaacs, a gifted educationalist who started an experimental school called the Maltings House School in Cambridge. Over a three-year period from 1924 to 1927 she kept detailed observation notes of the children at play. Her purpose was to throw light upon both the intellectual and the social development of these children. Her initial aim had been to write about both aspects in one book, but the material gathered revealed so much that she produced one whole volume focusing solely on intellectual development – the now famous *Intellectual Growth in Young Children*. This work, first published in 1930, is sadly out of print, but it provides fascinating reading, partly because the observations themselves, like those of Dibs, are revealing and moving, but also because Isaacs's analyses of what they show are fascinating.

Here are some examples drawn from the book in which Isaacs includes her detailed observations of what children said and did as they played, talked and learned.

At the end of the afternoon, Frank changed his jersey, shoes, etc because he was going out to tea. Dan (3; 7) noticing this, said, 'I'm having Mrs. I to tea – and that's why I have *this* jersey on'.

(Isaacs 1960: 145)

When modelling, Frank had made some railway lines. Paul asked him, 'What about the sleepers?' Dan answered, 'Ph, this kind of railway doesn't have sleepers.' Paul (4; 0) said, 'Oh, is this another country?'

(Isaacs 1960: 151)

5

You will be able to see how, through writing down everything seen and heard and then thinking about it, Susan Isaacs was able to start analysing children's intellectual development.

BECOMING A 'THINKING OBSERVER'

Susan Isaacs first trained as a teacher and later studied philosophy. She then went on to both study and practise as a psychoanalyst. So, in a sense, she has much in common with Axline in that they were both interested in children's thinking and in their feelings. You may be interested to note that in the 1930s she became an 'agony aunt' for childcare journals, including *Nursery World*, under the pseudonym Ursula Wise. Like Axline she was capable of writing both highly technical psychoanalytic papers and accessible texts.

We get the sense that Axline, working intensely with one child defined as being in need of help, used close observations in her play room, to build up an increasingly detailed and complex picture of Dibs in a range of play situations. Her intention was to understand more about what the child's behaviour told her about his past and how it was affecting his present. This psychoanalytic approach is also to be found in the work of people like Freud.

Isaacs, working with children in groups, wanted to observe them in whole situations, not in 'testing' situations, and it was her intention to understand each child as a whole child – one who laughs and cries, plays and argues, thinks and asks questions. Although she focused on both social and emotional development, understanding children's cognitive development became more and more important in her work.

For those working in classrooms, playgroups, daycare centres or other settings, observing children is what we do. We do it in the garden or playground, when the children work and play, when they arrive and leave, at lunch and snack times. Often we do it in much the same way that we watch people when we sit in a café or sit on a park bench. We take notice of what we see and hear and it sometimes entertains and amuses us and gives us things to comment on or talk about. You will be able to remember some of the funny things you have heard children say during the day and then commented on to your colleagues or others. Many childcare workers have been trained to observe children closely and do this as part of their everyday work.

The types of observations I have been talking about are observations 'on the hoof', which means they involve just taking note of what you see and hear as you go about your normal life in the setting. In order for observation to become a useful tool to you in terms of understanding the children you work with and planning for their learning and development, the whole process needs to become more conscious and more organised. You will need to think about the place of observation in the whole cycle of children's learning and development.

Mary Jane Drummond (1998) reminds us that young children's learning is fascinating to watch because it is so varied and surprising and enthusiastic and energetic and we can sometimes observe it unfolding before our eyes. Read the paragraphs below about Ozman to get an idea of what Drummond believes:

> Ozman is 5 and his current passion is for toys called Bey Blades. He can spend hours spinning the tops, tracking their paths, comparing one with another. Sometimes this play, totally engrossing, is silent, but sometimes he talks himself through it, making a running commentary about what he is thinking. A casual observer might conclude that he just loves Bey Blades. A thinking observer would begin to notice that the toys are just a vehicle for his interest in things that spin: in rotation itself. The thinking observer could only come to this conclusion through watching Ozman on different occasions, doing different things.

Here are some notes made about Ozman by his key worker:

> He took a pen and drew a series of circles and spirals on a piece of paper.
>
> Out in the playground he twirled round and round and then ran in large circles, followed by a friend.
>
> With his finger, in some flour spilled on the table, he drew a series of circular shapes.
>
> Became interested in the globe on a shelf in the corridor and kept spinning it round and round.

You can see how these small incidents, observed almost casually, offer anyone paying attention to Ozman's learning an insight into what it is that really interests him at the moment. The key worker, by noting down what she saw and heard, helped develop a complex picture of this one child as a learner.

Back to Drummond who helps us see that if we observe children attentively and thoughtfully we gain insights that are priceless when we start to think about learning and development. Ozman's teacher might notice that he likes to play with Bey Blades, and focus on helping him learn the alphabet by writing the letter B in his alphabet book. Or, if she had enough time to think about what it is about the Bey Blades that Ozman might be paying attention to – i.e. the fact that they rotate and spin – she might think about how to offer opportunities in the class for Ozman relating to rotation. Although she might plan activities specifically to meet Ozman's identified interests it is almost certain that other children would also be interested in spinning and rotation.

Observation, then, helps us to know more about individual children, and groups of workers can discuss who they want to watch, when and where. Here are some illustrations to show how different people do this:

▶ Marina talks about how, in their playground, they observe children who are new to the group and pay particular attention to how the children settle down, interact with other children or adults, use the space and cope with group activities or routines.

▶ Abi, in a nursery class, is interested in tracking the development of children across the six learning areas identified in the Foundation Stage Curriculum. She and her teaching assistant select four children to track each week.

▶ Maurice uses targeted observations of individual children in order to help him complete the Profile required of all teachers in reception classes in England. By targeted observations we mean observations of individual children doing specific things.

▶ Zohra is trying to ensure that three of the children who have English as an additional language are learning to understand and speak English. She does this by observing them involved in different activities in the nursery.

▶ Vanessa has a child in her group who displays very difficult behaviour in the daycare centre. Vanessa notes where and when this behaviour occurs, in an effort to understand what triggers it.

In each of these examples the adults are observing the children in order to find out more about some aspect of their learning or development. This will clearly affect whom they choose to observe and what they pay attention to.

Some sample observation notes made will illustrate this. Marina, the key worker, notes:

> Bobbi (3; 2) kisses mum goodbye – no crying – to book corner – looks at picture books alone 10 minutes – into garden onto trike – round and round, alone, 5 minutes – back inside – to Valerie (playgroup worker) – climbs on her knee (2 minutes) – taken to home corner – sets table, puts dolls on chair, dresses up; 2 other children there: no talk but lots of eye contact.

Abi, the nursery teacher, notes:

> Zac played in the workshop area today, making things out of junk materials. He made good choices and talked about what he was doing. He loves that area. He plays outside and looks at books. He is not very keen on domestic play and tends to be a loner.

Maurice, the reception class teacher, notes:

> Parveen can write simple sentence using developmental writing: no word boundaries: mixture of capital and lower case letters. Knows writing conveys meaning and some sound/symbol correspondence.

Zohra, the class teacher, notes:

> Abdul in book corner, sorting all the books by size and shape: listens to story and focuses closely on the story props; after story plays with props; goes over to Emma and tells her 'dog – boat' (pointing to the props).

Vanessa, the childcare worker, notes:

> Smiling as he came through the door. Rushed outside, up onto the climbing frame, played for 30 minutes. Onur tried to get on climbing frame. George kicked her. Brought inside by Denise and told to play quietly with the cars. Played for 5 minutes then rushed outside again and into the sandpit. Played with Josie, sharing moulds. Onur came over to join them. George very abusive and aggressive . . .

You can see how in each of these sets of observation notes what is recorded relates directly to what it was the thinking observer wanted to discover more about.

TAKING A CLOSER LOOK AT CLOSE OBSERVATION

Kate Pahl (1999) looked at children in a nursery setting and at home and used close observation as the tool for gathering evidence about their early literacy development. She explains in her book exactly what she did:

1   She chose to observe children in a nursery class where her own child was a pupil. In making this choice she ensured that the children would see her not as an outsider but as a parent who often came in and worked with them. She became a participant observer.

2   During her time in the nursery (two hours per week) she recorded everything that happened and took away some of the models and drawings made by the children or took photographs of what they produced.

3   She watched the children and took brief notes, which she then took home and wrote up in more detail. These became her observation notes or her working notes.

4   What she did next is very important. She read through the notes again and again and thought about what they told her or showed her about the children's developing understanding of literacy.

To summarise:

▷   She had a focus for her observation – to understand more about children's development in literacy.
▷   She became a participant observer.
▷   She recorded everything she heard and saw.
▷   She took notes and read them and reflected on them.

We begin to see a process emerging which shows just how the thinking observer uses observation as a valid and important educational tool. Pahl based her observation techniques on assuming that everything a child says or does is significant in building up a picture of his or her understanding of the world. This is called 'thick description'. Through recording everything seen and heard we begin to be able to answer some vital questions:

▷   What is this child paying attention to or interested in?
▷   What experience does the child have of this?
▷   What does the child already know about this?
▷   What does the child feel about this?

The answers we give cannot be said to be 'right', but attempting to answer these questions gives us the best possibility of knowing more about the child.

Pahl cites this example:

Lucy made a shopping basket out of an old tissue box. She made a handle and then wrote a list, which she stuck to the basket. When Pahl asked her what she was doing she said the writing was to show her mum. Pahl's analysis was that Lucy was able to make a link between her experience of going shopping and seeing shopping lists with the act of making a basket and attaching a piece of writing to it. 'The things that are linked in the mind have become linked in the material world.'

(Pahl 1999: 21)

Here is another example:

Ben wrote out a list of the names of countries, using his developing under-standing of the English written system. He asked me 'Can you read them?'

    sthaFGR
    TUCe
    UmeRC
    veenam
    itaL
    ᒋRDS

When his list was read several fascinating things emerged. First was that he drew together his current interest in writing lists of all sorts with his interest in beginning to be able to work out how to write words in English. Second was that the countries he had chosen to list all had some personal significance for him. He was born in South Africa and at the time he wrote the list his father was on holiday there. He had had a lovely holiday in the summer in the next country on the list – Turkey. America is much in the news at the moment and his best friend at school had missed the start of term because he was in America. And so on.

What more do we know about Ben after observing, scrutinising and reflecting? We can make a list:

▷ We know he is interested in becoming a writer and that he already knows how to use letter names and the sounds he is learning at school to produce words.

▷ He also knows that the words he writes are not correct, but is delighted that, despite that, people can often read them.

▷ From this we also know that he knows that writing means creating something that others can read.

▷ We know that he enjoys the organisation of lists – one word beneath another. He often makes lists of names of friends, shapes and so on.

▷ We know that he knows a lot about the countries in the world and that some of them have particular significance for him.

A few weeks after producing the list of countries Ben produced a sheaf of small pieces of paper, on each of which was written the name of one of the children in his class. Here he was using the concept of listing but organising it differently onto individual pieces of paper. Was he exploring whether a list has to be linear or whether it is still a list if it appears on separate pieces of paper? We can guess: only Ben knows the answer.

OBSERVATION AS A TOOL FOR UNDERSTANDING DIVERSITY

In previous sections we have looked particularly at how observing the children we work with can give a window into their social and intellectual development. Observation is also a crucial tool in getting to know more about the children you encounter. As early years workers you will already know that good practice means you must start with what the child already knows. In order to know what the child already knows you may need to use a range of tools or devices. One of these is observation.

In most playgroups, nurseries, classrooms or daycare centres throughout England there are diverse groups of children. There are obvious differences in terms of gender, age or ethnic group; there are less apparent differences in terms of the languages spoken, the cultures and religions, the values and aspirations, and there are deep and significant differences in life experiences.

Did you know that:

▷ there are more than 19 million refugees in the world today (US Committee for Refugees 1996)?

▷ in England one in eight children comes from a group defined as an ethnic minority group (Twigg 2003)?

▷ more than 630,000 children in England speak a first language other than English (Twigg 2003)?

▷ 82,000 children in England are refugees or asylum seekers (Twigg 2003)?

Tina Hyder (1998) tells us that there are proportionately more under-5s among refugees than among other groups and refugees are very likely to seek the services of daycare provision. So you are likely to come across children from refugee or asylum-seeking families, particularly if you work in the inner city. These statistics offer you some indication of the issues affecting all those working with young children, but it is very important to remember that when we talk about refugees or asylum seekers we are talking about as diverse a group as when we talk about 'English' people or '5-year-olds'. In other words, refugees are not a homogeneous group and it is important not to make any judgements or assumptions about the children who come to you on the basis of the label that they carry. Nonetheless, the experiences of refugee children – like all our experiences – have contributed to making them who they are, and knowing something about what they may have experienced will help you identify what you see when you observe them.

It is certain that all refugee children will have experienced loss. As Ron Baker (1983) puts it:

Loss of what is obvious, tangible and external such as possessions, a home, work, role, status, life style, a language, loved members of the family or other close relationships; and loss that is less obvious, 'internal' and 'subjective' such as loss of trust in the self and others, loss of self-esteem, self respect and personal identity.

Many children deal with these losses effectively, make relationships, learn a new language and succeed at school. But an awareness of what children might feel helps observers understand what they see or hear.

13

▶ Four-year-old K from Somalia came into the centre this morning, threw his coat on the floor, took a tin of pens and climbed up on the slide and threw the pens and the tin up in the air. When I brought him inside, explaining that he might have hurt someone, he went and sat in the home corner with his hands over his ears and wouldn't talk to me or look at me. His key worker said 'I thought about what we said at our staff development session and decided that his experiences have made him angry and afraid of the anger of other people. I try to be very calm now in my dealings with him and to never raise my voice.'

▶ Paolo, from Angola, drew soldiers and bombs all over a piece of paper. Then he went into the block play area and started throwing the blocks, making 'bang' noises. The nursery worker said 'We are fortunate in having someone in the centre who has been on a course about refugee children and she told me to try and make Paolo feel wanted in the centre and to try and involve him in all the activities, but not force him to do anything. I need to try and find someone who speaks Portuguese so that we can communicate with his mother.'

Penny Holland (2003) has written a controversial book in which she argues that the policies most settings have operated of zero tolerance towards playing with guns do little to promote the values they set out to promote. What do you make of this example?

In one centre the headteacher invested in a set of toy soldiers and action dolls. The staff were told not to stop the children engaging in war play or superhero play. In the nursery were two children, recently arrived from war-torn Congo. They had been anxious and withdrawn, not willing or able to engage with the other children or with the activities on offer. Gradually they began to play with the toy soldiers and the action dolls and it became apparent that they were using them to act out and represent some of their life experiences.

Taking note of what children do and say is the first step in the observation process. What comes next is thinking about what the evidence you have gathered suggests to you about the child. In order for this second step to be successful you need to use what you know about children's learning, about the individual histories of children, about the ways in which the languages spoken by the children work, about customs and values that are significant in the lives of the children. This is a tall order, but if you are to be a thinking observer it is something you need to do.

You need to know something about the languages of the children in your group or class if you are going to be able to understand what they are doing as they begin to read and write. If you know what the different scripts look like and the directions in which they are written you will better be able to understand children's early mark making.

To help you see this more clearly here are some case studies:

- ▶ Gaby, whose first language is Hebrew, looks at a picture book from what we would regard as the back of the book, turning pages till she reaches the 'front' of the book. What looks like random behaviour starts to make sense when you know that Hebrew is read from back to front.
- ▶ Sonay, a Turkish child, writing about her family, used the words 'sidren and brodren' to refer to her sisters and brother. Sonay's mum told the class teacher that the ending 'ren' is often added to plurals in Turkish.
- ▶ Abdul put a straight line on top of a string of letter-like shapes and 'read' what he had written. The Bengali-speaking language support teacher told the class teacher that his writing showed he was drawing on his experience of seeing Bengali script.

If you are not aware of what the languages of the children are or of some of the key features of the languages you will not be able to analyse your observations effectively.

If you are to understand what you see and hear you also need to know something about what is understood about how children learn and develop. We will come to that in the next chapter.

WHO OBSERVES WHOM?

If we can learn so much about children through observing them, might not they learn as much from observing both the adults around them and one another?

Barbara Rogoff (1990) has written about how children learn about the cultures in which they live through *their* observations of skilled adults or more skilled children. In many situations cited in her research the adults make no effort to 'teach' the children but the children themselves take responsibility for working out the essential features of an activity, and accommodating this into their existing understanding.

> In one of her books, she includes a photograph of a Mayan toddler in Guatemala, going with his mother to the market and watching as she bargains for a good price for a cabbage. What do you think this child is learning about his mother, the culture, economics, and social interactions?

> A second example shows a 5-year-old American child watching his father trying to fix a fishing reel. Rogoff suggests the child is learning about 'mechanics, fishing and cursing'.

It is clear that observation is a tool for learning to be used in many settings and by many people. Rogoff believes that children learn about real life through what she calls 'guided participation'. Here the child, alongside an adult or more skilled child, is inducted into the skills and routines of the cultural life of the group. An example shows that some children, who accompany adults to their work (babies on the backs of mothers in the fields, at the marketplace or pavement kitchen, beside their mothers at the weaving loom, or playing alongside the river), watch and become skilled at watching. Sometimes learners can participate in the process, as in Guatemala where Nash (1967) reports that adults learning to weave merely sit alongside a skilled weaver, asking no questions and being given no explanations. The learner may be asked to fetch a spool of thread but does not begin to weave until he or she feels competent to do so. At that point the apprentice becomes the skilled weaver. What this suggests is that skilled observation is an active and not a passive learning process. It is worth thinking about what, if any, opportunities we offer to children to become skilled observers themselves.

HAVING CONVERSATIONS

Julie Fisher (1999) argues that, in order to know as much as possible about the children, teachers (and other educators) need to become learners themselves. To do this they need to have what Fisher calls 'conversations' with those who can tell them what they need to know about the children. She is referring to parents, other adults involved in the lives of the children, and the children themselves. When she talks about 'conversations' she means genuine and equal exchanges between participants. Where the conversation is between child and adult, children can be invited to talk about and reflect on what they have been doing, what they have learned, what they enjoyed, what they found difficult and so on. Conversations like these are difficult to 'engineer' and they require that the adult set up an environment where children know that what they say is of genuine interest to the adult. It follows that conversations where the adult is questioning the child or testing the child cannot be seen as equal or genuine, and children are unlikely to reveal their feelings and thoughts.

Also revealing are the conversations children have in a group, sometimes when there is an interested adult involved. Here is an interesting example, taken from the work of Susan Isaacs:

> The rabbit had died in the night. Dan found it and said, 'It's dead – its tummy does not move up and down now'. Paul said, 'My daddy says that if we put it into water, it will get alive again'. Mrs. I said, 'Shall we do so and see?' They put it into a bath of water. Some of them said, 'It is alive'. Duncan said, 'If it floats, it's dead and if it sinks, it's alive.' It floated on the surface. One of them said, 'It's alive, because it's moving.' This was a circular movement, due to the currents in the water. Mrs. I therefore put in a small stick which also moved round and round and they agreed that the stick was not alive. They then suggested that they should bury the rabbit and all helped to dig a hole and bury it.
>
> (1960: 182–3)

SUMMING UP

In this chapter we have talked about how observation of children can and should be an indispensable tool in discovering what children know and can do. We have charted how the skilled observer listens and looks and records what is seen and heard. The thoughtful observer then draws on all that she or he knows about how children learn and develop to analyse these observation notes in order to make some judgement about what the child already knows, what the child is interested in or paying attention to, and what the child can do. We have thought about how observation helps us understand children whose experience includes things we are not familiar with – different languages, life experiences, values and ideas. We are ready to move on to looking at how observation provides the best basis for planning.

GLOSSARY

Close observation	This is observation which details everything the observer sees or hears.
Cognitive development	The development of thinking and reasoning, solving problems, communicating ideas. Also called intellectual or mental development.
Conscious	When something becomes conscious it means that it is something we are aware of.
Guided participation	Where children learn how to do things by observing closely what the adults or more skilled children do.
Managing behaviour	Usually refers to behaviour which is regarded as unacceptable and sometimes described as 'naughty'.
Observation	Taking careful note of everything said or done by a child or children over a defined period of time in a particular setting or context.
Participant observation	Where the observer is part of the setting or activity where the observation takes place.
Reflecting	Used in this chapter reflecting means thinking about.
Scrutinising	Looking carefully at something in order to understand more.
Targeted observation	Where the observer chooses a particular child or a particular activity or a particular time of day on which to focus the observation.
Thick description	A phrase introduced by Geertz (1973) to explain how in observation everything a child does is significant and deserves attention.

Chapter 2

Assessing learning

✔ In this chapter you will understand what is meant by assessment.

✔ You will understand that some assessment can be formative, some summative and some diagnostic.

✔ You will see how important assessment is in the learning process.

✔ You will think about how opportunities for assessment should be obvious in all activities, planned and spontaneous.

✔ You will think about whether assessment and testing are the same things or not.

DEFINING ASSESSMENT

Assessment is nothing new. Parents and carers, grandparents and siblings, do it as they watch children and respond to them according to what they see and hear.

▶ 'I think she is ready to have the stabilisers taken off her bike tomorrow' said Judy, after watching 5-year-old Ulgen whiz round the park. 'She is much more advanced physically than her sister was at that age.'

▶ 'Filiz would really like Elhamiye to come and play. They get on really well in school even though Filiz is older.'

▶ 'Darling mum, I am sending you a photo of the baby and you can see that he is very blond and beautiful, with lots of hair.

He is sitting up already! You will remember that Paolo didn't sit until he was 8 months old.'

▶   'I am teaching Leonardo to read, even though he is still not four. I am doing this because I want him to do really well when he starts in the reception class.'

▶   'I am really worried about Stephanie. She doesn't make eye contact at all and doesn't talk yet. I have an appointment to take her to the clinic tomorrow.'

In this selection of everyday comments made by parents about their children you can see that the parents are making some sort of judgement about something the child has done – or not done, as in the last case. Sometimes they refer to other children in the family and compare one child with another. They sometimes note progress by looking back at what the child could do before (as in the first example), or come to some conclusion about 'norms'. Doing this means comparing children with some notion of what the majority of other children of that age can do. In none of these examples is assessment done formally. It seems to be a commonsense way of thinking about children and helping them learn and develop.

Assessment as a formal process started with Susan Isaacs and developed sporadically in schools and other settings until 1990 when the Rumbold Report *Starting with Quality* suggested that educational provision for all 3- and 4-year-olds should be underpinned by careful assessment and recording procedures. The key thought in all of this is that assessment is a process and a complex one at that. It is something that is ongoing and changing – a dynamic and not a static thing. One way of thinking about assessment which is helpful is to regard it as the process of gathering together a body of evidence to help one make decisions about what a child knows and can do at a particular point in time. It is rather like what a detective does when trying to solve a case: gather together as much evidence as possible and then analyse it.

Assessment is used for a number of purposes. The most obvious one is the assessment that comes after the learning has taken place. This sort of assessment – called *summative assessment* – takes place at the end of a project, the end of a term or the end of the year. The idea is that the child is questioned, tested or assessed in some way in order to establish what he or she has learned. This kind of assessment is a summary of all that has been learned. The most obvious types of summative assessments are things like end-of-year reports, where parents are told what has been achieved over a term or a year. You might want to start thinking about what type of assessment is used when children are given Baseline Assessment tests or end of Key Stage tests.

The sort of assessment that you are all involved in all the time is called *formative assessment*. This is the on-the-job kind of assessment we all do all the time when working with children. Here are some examples:

▶ Rehana (4 years 4 months) tidying up in the home corner was matching the cups to their silhouette shapes on the shelf. The nursery nurse helping with the tidying up heard her say: 'six shapes, only four cups, two must be missing'. She noted in the child's file that on this occasion Rehana had been able to subtract mentally and commented that this was the first time it had happened.

▶ At story time a conversation developed about the languages spoken by the children and their families. Amina said 'My mum speaks English when she comes here but we speak Punjabi at home'. Sofia added 'I can speak English too – and Spanish. I speak Spanish with my grandma'. The teaching assistant asked if Sofia could tell her some words in Spanish and Sofia said 'Gracias – that's thank you'. 'I can say thank you in Italian' added the teaching assistant, and went on to note in the files of both children a growing awareness of knowledge about languages.

▶ In the reception class some magnets were set out on a table and the teacher was sitting with a group of children watching them play with the magnets and noting what they said. Although she had an idea in her own mind about what she wanted the children to learn from this activity (her learning intentions or outcomes) she noted down which children had met these and anything else interesting she observed: 'Dan seems to know a lot about magnets. He built towers of them and explored pushes and pulls.'

Built into many activities are opportunities for assessing what the children have learned and what they are paying attention to. When planning activities teachers will think carefully about how to offer such opportunities and will work with all the adults in the room to ensure that attention is paid to noting down what the children do and say.

A third purpose of assessment is *diagnostic*. Where someone has a concern about some aspect of a child's learning, behaviour or development, assessment may be used in order to try to identify what the cause of the difficulty is.

In short, the assessment you will mostly be involved in doing is formative assessment. You will do summative assessment occasionally (as when completing Baseline Assessments) and diagnostic assessment when you are trying to define more carefully something that is causing you concern.

PLANNING FOR ASSESSMENT: PLANNING FOR LEARNING

Teachers are involved in planning opportunities where children can be observed and assessed and this means that they must pay attention to planning how and where the adults in the room are deployed. This has implications for how children are taught and how they learn. Most settings recognise that learning is a very social activity and that children learn through their interactions with other children but also through their interactions with adults. This links to the work of Vygotsky which we will discuss later in this chapter. The careful planning of what the adults will do is an essential ingredient in successful teaching and learning. Fisher (1999) talks about three different types of activities that may be planned for children. These are **child-initiated** activities, where children are invited to follow their own interests through play in situations and tasks that have meaning and purpose for them; **teacher-initiated** activities, where the teacher has carefully planned what the children will be doing (as in the Literacy Hour, for example, where the teacher plans activities for groups of children not all requiring the constant presence of an adult); and **teacher-intensive** activities, where the planned activity requires the constant and intense presence of the teacher (or of another adult). An example of this could be the Guided Reading part of the Literacy Hour or the teacher reading to the children.

Adult time is precious in a class with twenty-eight or more children in it, and planning the use of this time requires much thought. In many settings teachers plan times when groups or individuals have access to adult time in intensive tasks while the rest of the children engage in child-initiated or teacher-initiated activities. The teacher plans that the adults move from one intensive activity to another. In good early years settings there is always much room for independent learning since promoting independence is so important in the early years. You will

know how difficult it can be to encourage children to work independently and not always seek the support, help and advice of an adult.
Good teaching ensures that help and advice are always available but that
children are encouraged to 'have a go'.

In many classrooms and even in some nurseries a plenary session is
planned to round off an activity or a session. This is where all the children come together to share what they have done and reflect on what
they have learned. This is not always appropriate for young children and
care should be taken to see that it is done with sensitivity. In some
nurseries the plenary session takes the form of a more friendly circle-
time where children are invited to talk about what they have been doing.

THE PLACE OF ASSESSMENT IN TEACHING AND LEARNING

You will probably have read or heard about the wonderful nursery
schools in an area of Italy called Reggio Emilia. These are famous because
of their clear focus on the children as active learners. Many of those
who have visited these nursery schools have tried to bring home with
them a notion of a Reggio Emilia 'curriculum'. There is no such
curriculum but there is much we can learn from what they are doing
in these nursery schools.

For example, in the nursery schools of Reggio Emilia all those
involved with children have an absolute belief in children's abilities to
use everything at their disposal to make sense of their world. In other
words they take for granted that young children are rich and powerful
thinkers. Educators, called 'pedagogiste', listen to children and watch
them and then document all their joint enterprises. By recording what
is seen and heard and assessing this, educators open up the possibilities
for genuinely responsive ways of teaching. This means that instead of
starting with some objective or outcome, educators start with what they
have seen the children do and say, and use this as the basis for planning
what is to come. Here are some examples:

> A child brought in a bus ticket after the long summer break and said
> that she had been to visit her grandmother and had seen 'lots of arms
> and legs'. The teacher followed this up and found out that the grand-
> mother lived in a hillside town where the route to the beach involved
> walking down very narrow streets lined with tall houses. You can imagine
> that the view for the small child was that of arms and legs. The incident

developed into a whole project where children explored the concept of 'a crowd' and did this through visiting the town square to look at a crowd; drawing one another and cutting out the figures to make a crowd; acting as a crowd and so on. The focus of the educators is to encourage children to express their ideas and their feelings in as many different ways as possible. They believe that learning is consolidated where children have opportunities to represent and re-represent (represent again) their thoughts and feelings. So children can draw or model or act or sing or dance or construct something in order to explore ideas.

Children commented that the birds in the playground looked 'bored'. This developed into the children discussing what would entertain the birds and they decided that the birds needed play equipment. They went on to talk about how they could make play equipment for the birds and how they would assess how successful their attempts had been. The children talked and made plans and designs on paper; constructed things out of found materials and wood; painted what they had made and then set up a rota of bird watchers to count how many birds used the little swing, how many the roundabout and so on.

Observation is a vital tool for effective teaching and learning. It gives us a starting point by providing some evidence about where the child is at a particular point in time. From this starting point we can begin to make judgements. We do this in a number of ways:

1   We can make a judgement about the child based on our knowledge of other children of the same age, at the same stage, doing the same task, for example. In order to do this we need some knowledge of child development. Even with that it may be a tricky thing to do because, as you well know, all children are different and develop at different rates. A child's interests will certainly impact on how well he or she 'does' relative to other children. This type of judgement can be described as **normative** – i.e. informed by what it is thought that other learners of the same age know or can do.

2   We can make a judgement about the child based on our knowledge of *that* child. This requires us to have some in-depth knowledge of the child and this comes through our observations and interactions. Doing this enables us to make judgements about the child's progress. The question we ask

is 'Has this child moved on?' This kind of judgement is **formative** in the sense that it is ongoing and helps us plan what to offer next.

3   In our educational system we are increasingly asked to make judgements about a child in relation to some pre-determined learning outcome or goal. So we might plan an activity for the children to do and have a set of learning outcomes in mind. These could include things like 'use a pair of scissors effectively' or 'use fine motor control well'. We would watch what the child does or what the child produces and then tick a box. Although this is a growing trend in early years education in England it is important to remember that in any situation the outcomes you have in your mind for what you want the children to learn may not match what the children want to learn. So this type of **outcomes-based** assessment gives an imperfect picture.

We know that observation and assessment can give us insights into what the child knows and can do at any point in time. But observation and assessment must also point to the future. Knowing what the child can do now allows us to plan the next step in learning for that child. The great Russian theorist Vygotsky noted that any observation of a child gives a picture of the child's performance at that time but that this is a limited picture. The child's potential to move ahead is missing. Vygotsky called this the 'zone of proximal development' – i.e. where the child could be in his or her learning with help. So Vygotsky believed that assessment is the starting point, and for it to be important in the learning and teaching process it needs to point to learning potential. He believed that learning directed towards what the child can already do or already knows is ineffective. The child cannot learn what he or she already knows. Learning takes place where the child takes the next step in the learning process.

Vygotsky was interesting in many ways, not least because he believed that learning is an immensely social process. This means that learning takes place primarily through the interactions learners have with more able learners who may be adults or other children. In his writings Vygotsky indicates that children demonstrate two developmental levels. The first is the one mentioned above where the child's performance (what she or he does or says) reveals the actual developmental level; the second is their potential developmental level – what they could do with help. It is the gap between these two levels that is the zone of proximal development.

On first reading, these may seem to be complicated ideas but they do make complete sense once you understand them. Perhaps an example will help.

► Joe (5; 8) reading a book gets stuck on the word 'cake': the adult says 'Remember that "magic e" rule I told you about?' Joe immediately reads the word correctly.

► His performance level (not able to read the word cake) was 'lower' than his potential level (able to do it with help).

UNPICKING THE CYCLE

The cyclical nature of observation, assessment and learning should now be beginning to appear. We said that observation and documentation provide a starting point. Then assessment, or making judgements against what has been seen or heard, allows us to interpret where the learner is and to start to think about how to help the child take the next step in learning. So the next step in the cycle is planning. So we have observation–documentation–assessment–planning.

To illustrate this, let's track what was said by a range of nursery workers at a recent workshop on planning:

Abiola said 'The headteacher insists that we must plan for the medium term and for the long term. We are, of course, working within the Foundation Stage and towards the Early Learning Goals. Some of us feel anxious about the pressure on us to plan, plan and plan. We fear that there will be an imbalance with too much adult-directed work and the loss of children's flexibility and ability to choose. And we are all really, really committed to ensuring that our children learn best through play. We spent much of last year trying to understand what made play so important as a mode of learning and what we now understand is that play must be self-chosen to enable children to take risks and learn from their own "doing".'

Tahiba added 'I think we can still plan and allow children to make choices. We can plan to resource and staff the six learning areas, using some-thing of a workshop approach. So if we make sure we provide easily accessible resources for children to use to follow their own agendas we are both planning and not stifling free choice. This means we know that children learn best through play and we encourage this.'

Mark said 'I agree. At my centre we do that well in the creative workshop with all the resources we have for making models, cutting and sticking, painting and drawing, and so on. We also do it well in the writing workshop area where we have lots of materials to stimulate writing – paper, envelopes, pencils, rubbers, stickers, blank books, alphabets on display.'

Emily told the group that her headteacher had visited the nurseries in Reggio Emilia and been impressed by the 'thematic' approach. 'We plan around themes and we get the themes from observing what children are interested in and then setting up areas of the room to support these interests. I know it might seem that we are only meeting the needs of those children whose interests we develop, but in reality we take note of who plays in the areas we have set up and find that they usually meet a wide range of needs. We have had a very strange range of themes. We had a shoe shop because one child was obsessed with a new pair of trainers. That gave us lots of opportunities for mathematics – pairs, measuring feet, sorting things out, pricing objects. Then we had "Spinning" in response to a class craze for Bey Blades. That offered opportunities for science and mathematics and literacy and – well, everything really.'

Cathy added another dimension to the discussion when she talked about her nursery class's focus on building on children's interests. 'We have had a strong focus on schemas and have involved parents in this. We look carefully to try and find things that children are very interested in and that are displayed as repeated behaviours. You know the sort of thing. The child who is forever transporting things from one part of the room to another. Or the child who hides things in the sand, covers over a beautiful picture with a layer of black paint. We then try and provide opportunities for children to follow their own particular interests within the context of the rich resourcing in different areas of the room.'

Babette told the group about her reception class's focus on 'match'. 'Our early years coordinator went on a course about planning and came back to talk to us about how we change things round too often. She said that when we do that we don't encourage children to get very involved in what they are doing. We encourage them to just move from one thing to another. She said we have low expectations of what children can do and she has given us a paper to read about the Theory of Match. This says we should put out an activity and watch how the children use it. When the play gets static or the children don't want to play there any more we should add something to the activity or take something away. What we add or take away should be something small. The idea is that the children will be interested in the change and start exploring in that activity all over again. If we offer a change that is too big or not related to what the children were exploring we will lose their attention. I have been trying this, particularly in our workshop area and it is amazing. Children will spend hours on end making models just because I have added some circular shapes or some paper clips or something else to the materials already on offer.'

SQUARING THE CIRCLE

In order for planning to be based on observation and assessment, workers working together need to meet and talk. Many settings have a brief but focused meeting at the end of each day where individual staff members report back on what they have seen individual children or groups of children doing. On the basis of this, decisions are made about what to make available the next day. If nobody played with the dinosaurs in the dry sand, perhaps wet sand should be provided. If children were unhappy at story time because they had not finished what they were doing in the construction area, perhaps the same things should be available the next day. This brief planning meeting seems an essential feature of responsive planning and, if properly managed, is neither lengthy nor onerous.

So we have the cycle:

The observation–documentation–assessment–discussion–planning–observation cycle

1 looking at and listening to what is said and done;
2 documenting this (writing it down);

3   reading through it and thinking about what it reveals (drawing on what you know about the individual child and about children in general);
4   sharing your thoughts with others;
5   agreeing what to plan for individual children the next day.

Having worked through all of the five points above you start the whole process again. You can see that it is a cycle. As you implement the plans you made, you watch and listen to see if you got it right and you notice what the children are now doing and saying. You start observing the children again to see what they now know and can do.

ASSESSMENT AND TESTING

Because of the pressures on all educators to both assess and test children there is some confusion about what is meant by these terms. Is assessment the same as testing or are the two quite different? A recent article in the *Guardian* (17 April 2003) stated that: 'Children are being railroaded into a testing culture that squeezes out the joy of learning and turns schools into "factories".'

At the annual conference of the Association of Teachers and Lecturers, in Blackpool, national tests for children aged 7, 11 and 14, the number of exams for the A-level curriculum, and the pressures on children aged 3 to 5 were mentioned as likely to make pupils feel like failures. The President of the Association said that many children are turned off learning because they are bored by being offered a curriculum with little choice or relevance to their lives. He went on to ask:

> What sort of education system do we have if we brand children as failures by the time they are 11, or worse, 7? What sort of morality is it to force on young children an impoverished curriculum diet just to help politicians meet targets and keep the Treasury happy? What difference does it really make to a child's life if he or she achieves [certain levels] aged 11? Will it really make them a better person, a genuinely enriched human being with a passion for learning? Of course it won't.

Educationalists do not argue with the importance of assessment as long as it is assessment designed to help children learn. What people are complaining about is that the curriculum – even for the youngest children – is being driven by national tests, resulting in league tables.

Some people believe that one of the difficulties is the fact that our children still start formal schooling at an earlier age than anywhere else in the world and, with the curriculum so tightly controlled by top-down pressures, the opportunities for them to follow their own interests or to get deeply involved in solving problems or expressing ideas and feelings become fewer and fewer. The result is the many very young children who don't want to go to school, don't find joy in reading, and who begin to exhibit difficult patterns of behaviour and lack self-esteem.

You may be interested in an article that appeared in the *Education Guardian* on 16 September 2003, entitled 'Heaven and Helsinki'. The article was about schools in Finland and about what Britain could learn from how the Finns organise their education system. One of the features is that pre-schooling starts when children are 6, when they attend a kindergarten. Formal education starts a year later and they remain in the same school until they are 16, when they move on to a lukio (an upper secondary school) or to a vocational school for three years. The headteacher of one school commented, 'It's wonderful to see the children grow up. Half of the kids will be able to read by the time they get here at 7 years old. For those who can't we offer remedial help.' There is no streaming and no selection. The private sector is very small, so almost all children attend state schools. Alongside this there is an almost complete absence of formal exams and national testing. All children take one national exam at the end of the lukio – their first national exam. The Finns say that they do not create league tables of good and bad schools. What is impressive is that in the OECD/Unesco (2003) report on education Finland had the best reading scores; and in mathematics it was the leading European country. What is, perhaps, most interesting is that the socio-economic makeup of the school has less effect on results than anywhere other than Israel and Norway.

These are important issues to think about. We have no solutions but it is a debate worth having with your friends and colleagues.

SUMMING UP

In this chapter we have looked at the different types of assessment and the different reasons for having them. This led us into seeing that observation is the starting point for the whole assessment process, which moves from observation (what we see and hear) to analysis (what this tells us about the child's learning), to planning (what we must now offer that child or children), to observation again (what we see and hear in the new activity or situation), to analysis (what this shows about the child's learning) and so on. We have started to look at how educationalists must set up workable systems for observing children and assessing their progress. Questions have been raised about the differences between assessment and testing.

GLOSSARY

Assessment	The process of gathering together evidence of what a child already knows and can do.
Cyclical	Something that follows on from another until a circle is completed and the whole process starts again.
Diagnostic assessment	The process of trying to identify something you think might be wrong.
Documentation	The process of writing down your observations and your assessments.
Formative assessment	The process of taking regular note of what children say and do as they play and learn. This is then used as the basis for planning and for giving feedback to the learner.
Learning areas	The Foundation Stage Curriculum in England defines the curriculum as being divided into six learning areas. Details can be found in the Foundation Stage documents or on the DfES website.
Norms	The concept that a majority of children at particular ages can do particular things. The norm is defined as what 'most children' can do. This is then used when one child is compared with a whole cohort – as in many testing situations.
Objectives or outcomes	These refer to the sorts of goals educators have when they plan or teach something.

Zone of proximal development	Vygotsky believed that there was a gap between what a child could do alone and what the child might do with help. This gap is known as the zone of proximal development or ZPD.

Chapter 3

The search for the significant moment

> ✔ In this chapter you will start to think about what sorts of things are important to record.
>
> ✔ You will be able to define what constitutes a significant moment in terms of learning and development.
>
> ✔ You will understand something about what is known about how young children learn best.
>
> ✔ You will get an insight into how to make assessment systems manageable.

A SYSTEM FOR ASSESSMENT

You may be working in a setting where you have no clear system for assessment and are thinking about putting one in place. Or you may work in a situation where there is a system, but it is cumbersome and difficult to manage. Here is one such system.

The headteacher has told all teachers to ensure that, in all classrooms, children are assessed at least once per week and in all areas of learning. In the reception class there are thirty children, two members of staff and six learning areas. Try as they might, the staff cannot manage to do anything other than tick off on a checklist what activities each child has been involved in over the week. This cannot really be described as assessment since it gives little useful information about what the children know and can do. It merely says that on such and such a day John, Giuseppe and Gurdeep all joined in a cutting and sticking activity, for example.

Another interesting example comes from a reception class in a different school where the teacher was struggling to track children's development as readers. What the early years coordinator advised her to do was to write down the titles of all the books chosen and 'read' by each child. The teacher did this for one term but when she looked through each child's reading record she realised that the information she had was of little use. Through discussion with colleagues in other settings she decided that what she needed to do was record anything significant that each child said or did with regard to reading.

That sounds quite straightforward and makes a lot of sense. But when she started looking for things to take notice of she realised that she needed a clear picture in her head of what sorts of things happen when children become readers. She asked herself if there was a sequence or a pattern of things to look out for. After reading articles about how children become readers she was able to make a list. Her list included things like this:

► Knows the front and back of the book
► Knows that the writing is read (in English) from left to right and from top to bottom
► Knows that you can read the pictures and the words
► Knows that when you read the words they always say the same thing
► Recognises some words (like own name)
► Knows lots of stories and rhymes
► Can re-tell a story in the right sequence
► Can predict what is going to happen
► When makes a mistake goes back to re-read and correct

You can see that this teacher has made a memory jogger, or a checklist of things to look out for. These things seemed to this teacher – and to many others, too – to be milestones on the road to being a reader. The checklist is not an exhaustive one. There are many other things you would want to take notice of or look out for. But it gives you an idea of what sorts of things we might define as significant moments.

RECORD-KEEPING

Keeping records must have a purpose and must be achievable. One way of making it both is to think about recording significant achievements.

A significant achievement may be defined as a leap in learning or development or progress. Many of you will be familiar with the developmental milestones that you may have used with regard to your own children: the eruption of the first tooth, the first word, the first step and so on. So a significant achievement will often be the first time you notice that a child can do something. But it might also be the first time you are sure that a child has fully grasped a concept because you see it used in different situations or contexts.

Here are some examples to illustrate this:

▶ Example 1
The first time Rehana tried to write her name she wrote R.;
the nursery nurse recorded this as a significant achievement:
'21st April 2002: Rehana wrote R for her name'.
Three months later Rehana wrote her name in full and this was recorded.
After that no one bothered to record that Rehana could write her name because, having done so once, it was clear that this was something she could do.

▶ Example 2
Joel was very shy on entry to the nursery. The teacher asked all staff to watch him for signs of beginning to interact with others.
23/02/02 Joel and Jerome played alongside one another in the blocks and Joel helped Jerome build a tower.
2/05/02 in singing today Joel came to the front for the first time.
3/06/02 in the playground Joel was the leader of a large group of children playing 'explorers' on the climbing frame.

You will see that the second example builds a picture of the child's confidence developing over a period of time.

Vicky Hutchin (2000) talks of there being five categories into which significant achievements might fall. These are physical skills, social skills, attitude development, conceptual development and process skills. Examples of each might make this clearer.

▷ Physical skills would include the use of tools and large motor skills – running, climbing and so on. They correspond to the Physical Development learning area.

▷ Social skills would include things like joining in, taking turns, sharing and so on. These fit neatly into the learning area of Personal and Social Development.

▷ Attitude development would include things like self-esteem, increasing confidence, growing independence. This does not feature as a learning area in the Curriculum Guidance to the Foundation Stage.

▷ Conceptual development would include developing ideas about print, about numbers, about the world, etc. This broad and important area would include Communications, Language and Literacy, Knowledge and Understanding of the World and Mathematical Development.

▷ Process skills refer to things like the ability to make predictions, to plan, to experiment. These vital skills are not identified *per se* in the Curriculum Guidance to the Foundation Stage but refer to skills vital to all learning areas.

Hutchin's scheme, which pays no attention to creative development, is only one way of organising significant achievements. For those of you working within the Foundation Stage Curriculum it would make more sense to relate the significant achievements to the six learning areas.

WHAT WE KNOW ABOUT YOUNG CHILDREN'S LEARNING

In order to know what a significant achievement is we need some clear idea of how young children learn. It is only with this in our heads that we have some reference points. If you go back to the example of the teacher trying to find significant moments in literacy at the beginning of this chapter you will see how important it was for the teacher to know what the progression from being an emergent reader to being a reader might look like. It was only knowing this that enabled her to develop pointers to look out for. The same applies to all learning.

You will know that young children are busy learning all the time. They take notice of everything they encounter and try to make sense of it. It is as though they continually ask themselves questions: What is this thing? What does it do? What can I do with it? Many of those who have studied learning in the past have described this search for meaning as the child being an *active learner*. The word 'active' is used to describe what is happening in the child's brain and does not imply that the learning only takes place when the child is physically active. So people like Piaget and Vygotsky, both of whose work has been very influential on all Western educators, believed that children often are in control of their own learning as they try to make sense of their world and their experiences. Piaget and Vygotsky are often described as 'constructivists' because what they say is that the child constructs a model of the world in his or her head and changes and adapts this in response to experiences. This is an active process – hence the child is an active learner.

Many things are important in the child's struggle and these include, most importantly, other people. All children live in a world with other people – in a social world. And their learning takes place in this social world. It makes perfect sense then to accept what Vygotsky tells us, which is that other people play a vital role in children's learning and development. Children learn from more experienced learners. They learn, of course, from their parents and grandparents and from their teachers and educators. But they also learn from other children. We can say that children learn through *social interactions*. You will remember that we talked about the 'zone of proximal development' earlier in this book and described this as the gap between what a child could do alone and what the child could do with help. In your search for significant moments you might be looking for the first time the child does something unaided (e.g. the first time a child puts on her shoes, the first time a child joins in a group activity), but also sometimes looking for evidence that the child has done more with help than she could do alone. Here is an example to illustrate this:

Six-year-old Stephanie made a circuit using light bulbs after looking at some illustrated books about electrical circuits. She was pleased with it and took it outside to show the class teacher. Out in the bright sunlight she commented that 'it's not working any more'. The class teacher stopped what she was doing when she recognised that Stephanie had found a problem to solve. 'Take it inside and try again, Stephanie', she suggested. The child duly took the circuit inside, tried it and came out to report 'It does work inside, but not out here'. 'I wonder why not', mused the teacher. 'I think it's because I can't see it out in the sun', said the child. 'I think it is working but not brightly.' 'Can we test it?' asked the teacher. Stephanie looked around the playground and spotted the play tent in which some children were playing on the grass. She took the circuit over, tried it out and came back satisfied.

Can you see how this skilled teacher was able to lead the child, step by supported step, to a point where she was able to solve a problem?

This type of intervention is known as *'scaffolding'* and it comes from the work of Bruner. The term 'scaffolding' suggests a support, just like the scaffold you would find on a building being renovated or restored. The scaffold is in place until the work is complete and the building will stand unaided. Scaffolding learning means helping the child move from one position to another – to fulfil their potential or make a leap in learning. Scaffolding helps the child move from being able to do something they could do with help to being able to do the same thing independently.

You will be able to see how this contributes to gathering evidence of significant moments.

Many theorists and educationalists believe that children learn best through *play*. What this means is that children learn best when they are able to follow their own interests. A child who arrives in the morning with a burning desire to make a book or build a fort or play out something that happened at home is able to explore his or her own concerns and become deeply involved. The child can take chances and make mistakes and cannot fail. If the fort collapses the child can start again or abandon it or call for help. So children, in self-chosen activities, take risks and taking risks is an important part of learning. Of course, adults need to be alert to what children are doing in their play and need to offer objects or advice or physical help to enable the child to move forward. Adults might want to get involved in a genuine dialogue with the child about what the child is doing, but asking questions to test the child sometimes destroys the play and the learning.

Recent readings of Vygotsky's work – much of which has not been available in English until recently – suggest that his zone of proximal development was not confined to the gap between what a child could do unaided and what the child could do with help, but could be defined as what the child reveals he or she can do through play. Famously, Vygotsky talked of a child standing 'a head taller than himself' when engaged in imaginative play. You may know that, for Vygotsky, play was the primary mode of learning, by which he meant that it was the way in which young children learned most successfully. He believed that through play children bring together many of their experiences and thoughts and feelings and combine these in new ways. This explains why some theorists talk of play as an 'integrating mechanism'. When you really watch a child at play you become aware that the child knows much more than might seem apparent when he or she is watched in other activities. So in your search for significant moments, do remember that imaginative play is a rich source.

Some scenarios will make this clearer:

Nigel Hall (1999) describes a project carried out in a nursery class where the class had turned part of the room into a library. The play had gone on for many weeks but the teacher decided that the play was getting static and wanted to change the area. Instead of just doing this on her own she involved the children through their imaginative play. She wrote a letter to be delivered to the nursery and read it aloud to the children when it was 'delivered'. The letter informed the children that the library had to close down by a certain date because the council did not have enough money to keep it open. The children, devoted to their classroom library, were distressed and when the teacher read aloud a sentence inviting them to write to the council if they wanted to say anything about the proposed closure, they became very animated and spent hours talking and discussing and having a go at writing. Of course, they were not able to write correctly, but many of them brought together all that they knew about writing and made marks on paper – often using recognisable letters, writing from left to right, adding their names at the end. They were able to 'read' these letters to the teacher, who was amazed to see how much they knew. Through their imaginative play they integrated aspects of their previous experience, their skills and their knowledge and showed themselves standing 'a head taller' than the teacher had realised.

In another example Hall (1999) describes the setting up of a garage in the nursery and a prolonged imaginative play sequence involving mechanics coming into the nursery, children estimating the cost of repairing bikes and examining the bikes to find what needed repairing. In this sequence it is clear that the project helped children, through their play and discussions, to come to understand more about how the world works. Again, when you read what the children said and did you are amazed at what they reveal.

Also important in learning is the role of *talk and language*. Think about how young children acquire their first language and, with a bit of thought, you will appreciate that this does not happen only through imitation – although this is what people used to believe. Something more exciting is going on and this offers evidence that children are not only active learners but also brilliant thinkers. In all cultures, in all languages, children go through a phase where, after having got things right through imitation, they start to get things wrong through thinking. In English, for example, most children at first get plurals right. Having heard people talk about cows and sheep and ducks they talk about cows and sheep and ducks. But at the age of about 2 (although this varies hugely) children will stop saying cows and sheep and ducks and will start talking about cows and sheeps and ducks. What is happening here is not that the children have suddenly become stupid. The children have worked out that there is a rule in English: the rule is that when we talk about plurals we add an 's' to the end of nouns: cows and ducks. The child then applies that rule to all situations. Now you and I know that there are rules and that there are also exceptions to rules. Children don't yet know this, so they go through this phase of overgeneralising rules – which means that they apply the rule to all situations. Knowing this will help you recognise that when a child makes an error of this type, it is, in fact, a milestone or a significant moment.

Children learn, then, through being curious and questioning and through language. They also learn through *exploration*. Watch a young child with a new object. The child will explore the object as thoroughly as possible. For young children this might mean putting the object in their mouth. For others it might mean shaking, touching, pushing or dropping the object. Go back to the first chapter and read some of the observation notes made by Susan Isaacs for evidence of children as young explorers. When you see a child dropping things over and over again, stop and ask yourself the question: What is this child trying to find out?

Children will learn best in situations where they can see the point of what they are being asked to do. Margaret Donaldson (1978) talked about the importance of children being in situations which are *meaningful* to them. Donaldson believed that much of what children are asked to do in schools makes little or no sense to them. They cannot see why they are being asked to fill in missing numbers or colour shapes in particular colours. Donaldson believed that young children, in particular, need to be in learning situations where they can draw on their past experiences and where they can see the purpose of the activities.

You might want to ask yourself which of the following situations is likely to make what Donaldson called 'human sense' to the child:

▶ Situation 1: in a work book the child is asked to colour in all the dogs green, cats pink and ducks orange.

▶ Situation 2: in the workshop areas there are pots of materials sorted by colour and available for the child to use to make collages.

Both invite the child to explore colour but in the first the child might ask 'Why am I doing this? What is the point?' Whereas in the second it is possible that selecting the materials and colours to make something of the child's own choosing will offer some challenges to the child which are meaningful. It is most likely that you will see the child in a significant moment in a situation which makes human sense to the child. Good early provision ensures that such situations occur throughout the setting.

Children learn through many experiences, including through books and stories and rhymes; through outings and walks and visits; through looking at pictures and objects and artefacts; through being engaged in real-life pursuits like planting and cooking. Some teachers use these experiences to help children *represent and re-represent* what they think and see and feel. In other words, after children have listened to stories or been on outings or handled objects there may be opportunities for the children to draw or paint; to make things out of clay or found materials or woodwork; to make up stories; to act things out; to play musical instruments or make masks or dance. This is the philosophy of the great nursery schools in Reggio Emilia, where the educators say that children have 'a hundred languages'. In England we tend to split the curriculum up into subject areas (like the learning areas), and although this is better than splitting the curriculum up into subjects (history, geography, etc.) it is not as sound as recognising that, for young children, learning is *holistic*. In the nursery schools in Reggio Emilia children have a group experience, such as going to the village square or on an outing to see the grapes growing, and then come back into the nursery and have opportunity after opportunity to express this experience. The walls are covered in children's paintings and drawings, their sketches and masks. Children are to be found making constructions and using computers and creating plays. They are representing their ideas and then, perhaps, re-representing them in a different mode or medium. Each representation may mark a significant moment as children refine their understanding.

One of the things recognised by educationalists in Reggio Emilia is the importance of what is called *affect* in learning. Affect refers to things like habits, attitudes, feelings or dispositions. You will know from your own experience that when learners feel positive about something and positive about themselves, learning is quicker and happier. Think about yourself learning something you really want to learn in a situation where you feel respected and confident. Contrast that with learning something you have not chosen to learn in a situation where you feel awkward. This is something most of us have experienced. If this is true for us, surely it must be true for children.

> Hannah goes to a music class after school. At this class she plays her violin in a string group and if she can't manage something she has learned to 'fake it'. She knows that no one will pick her out and that she can go home and practise so that next time she will manage. She is comfortable and confident. When a new teacher arrived at the group and wanted the children to dance and sing she refused to join in. She has little confidence when it came to things like movement and dance and her whole demeanour changed.

Affect is something we often pay too little attention to. Think about how some assessment tasks and situations affect children's confidence and self-esteem. Seven-year-old Thando arrived on the first day of Key Stage 1 SATS in floods of tears. Through weeks of repeated practice she had learned that she finds the tests difficult and what she is experiencing is failure. Just as Hannah in the example above could not engage with movement and dance because of her own sense of inadequacy, Thando (along with many other children) will find the testing situation involved in national tests something that makes her feel like a failure. You have probably all heard of the 'self-fulfilling prophecy'. This states that the more someone feels like a failure the more they will continue to fail. Building self-esteem and self-confidence are crucial aspects of teaching and learning and when we are looking for significant moments we should seek to assess children in situations where they feel comfortable and confident.

ONE FOR ALL?

You might be tempted to think that you can look for significant moments for a whole group of children, but the reality is that each child will demonstrate different significant moments. Here are some examples to illustrate this:

► Example 1
Sukvinder and Dillip started in the reception class at the same time and are firm friends. They play together in the classroom and in the playground and go and play in one another's houses after school. Despite their friendship the two children are very different in terms of both their interests and their experiences. Dillip loves drawing and painting and her drawings are detailed, highly patterned and very colourful. Sukvinder is more tentative and rarely chooses to draw. So when both girls were in the 'office' set up in the classroom and Sukvinder did a large poster using thick felt pens to make patterns around the edge, this was a significant achievement. For Dillip, doing something similar was not significant since she had previously and often demonstrated the skills being seen in Sukvinder's work. When Sukvinder looked at Dillip's poster and commented 'Wow! You've used so many colours and made it look really beautiful', this was a significant moment in terms of Sukvinder's social development.

► Example 2
Halil and Filiz are looking at a book together in the playgroup. Both are 4 and are nearly ready to move on to the reception class. Both are excited and nervous. Halil is not usually interested in books and stories, whereas Filiz recognises her name, the names of other children in the class and some key words. Her mother 'reads' with her every evening. So when Halil, looking at the book, starts to re-tell the story, the playgroup worker feels this is a significant moment. She says to Halil's mum 'Today, for the first time, he re-told a story in one of our books.' Two days later she heard Filiz re-tell the same story, but noticed that she was paying close attention to the words on the page and running her finger underneath them. This, for her, was a significant moment.

SUMMING UP

In this chapter we have looked at the importance of knowing something about how young children learn in order to enable us to recognise significant moments in learning.

We have examined the following features of early learning:

✔ How children are active learners and construct models of the world in their minds. These models are not fixed but change through experience.

✔ We have looked at the importance of social interactions in learning and we have seen how children learn both from the support of adults – particularly when they are able to scaffold learning – and from observing and imitating more expert peers.

✔ We have paid attention to play as the primary mode of learning. We have defined play as children being in charge of their own learning through following their own interests, getting deeply involved, taking chances, getting things wrong, changing the agenda in response to what is happening.

✔ We have seen how talk and language are crucial elements in many learning situations and how young children tend to spend much time in exploring objects and events they encounter.

✔ We have paid heed to Donaldson's advice about the importance of learning activities making human sense to children.

✔ We have considered the ideology of the nurseries in Reggio Emilia where children are invited to represent and re-represent their developing ideas and feelings in many ways, through different modes, using different resources.

✔ We have looked at the importance of self-esteem/confidence in successful learning.

✔ And finally we have reminded ourselves that young children do not learn in separate subjects, but holistically.

GLOSSARY

Active learning	The idea of the child being very curious and doing everything possible to understand the world.

Affect	Attitudes or dispositions which are very important in learning. The way you feel affects how you learn and what you achieve.
Checklist	This is a list of goals or targets that can be ticked off when the learner has been observed to have achieved them.
Developmental milestones	These are the notable things achieved by children as they move through life. The analogy of a journey is used so that each step along the road is seen as a milestone. Examples are children's first steps, first words, etc.
Exploration	The process of being an active learner by exploring everything in order to find out more. Synonymous with investigation.
Holistic	This means seeing things as a whole. For young children learning does not take place in subjects but as a whole.
'Hundred languages'	A phrase used by the educators in Reggio Emilia to describe what they do to allow children to use every means possible to express their ideas and thoughts and feelings.
Imaginative play	Sometimes called pretend play, this is when children try out different roles as part of being active learners.
Integrating mechanism	A system for bringing together many different things. Play is often described as an integrating mechanism because it allows learners to bring together what they already know and, from that, produce something new.
Meaningful	Something that makes sense. The best learning opportunities allow learners to see the point of what they are doing. They build on existing knowledge and experience and help move children from the real to the abstract.

Play	Difficult to define simply. It is a mode, or a way, of learning where the learner is in control of what it is that he or she wants to do. This allows the learner to become very involved and to take risks. And it is an integrating mechanism which allows us to see just how much children know and can do.
Representing	Children, as active learners, try to represent what they think and feel. In the nurseries in Reggio Emilia they are offered many different ways of doing this – writing, drawing, miming, acting, building, etc.
Scaffolding	A term taken from building and used by Bruner to describe how adults can help children's learning by supporting them in taking carefully paced steps from dependence to independence.
Social interaction	The process whereby people interact with one another. It is seen, by many, as an essential feature of much learning.

Chapter 4

Giving feedback

- ✔ In this chapter you will think about what to do with your observations to help the child move on.

- ✔ You will have some opportunities to reflect on how the feedback given by educators in some examples will help the children.

- ✔ You will refine your skills of being able to give really targeted and developmental feedback, both written and verbal.

- ✔ You will explore the current debate about the importance of praise in learning.

WHAT IS MEANT BY FEEDBACK?

It is interesting to think about where the term 'feedback' comes from because some of its roots are helpful in understanding its importance in learning. You will know that there are some simple feedback loops in things like thermostats which control temperature. There are also feedback loops within the human body and, most importantly, within the human brain. In the human nervous system such feedback loops control things like body temperature or blood pressure or fine motor movements. Much, much more complex feedback loops are also present in the brain and some theorists argue that these are responsible for memory and higher-order thinking.

One of the things that we, as human beings, can do is create 'scenes' in our minds, drawing on (a) what we have experienced; (b) language; (c) symbols; and (d) interactions with people. We are then able to reflect on all of these to create new understandings. This process involves:

1   integrating our experiences (and you will remember that play is often described as an integrating mechanism, suggesting that this is the way in which we bring together all our experiences); and

2   having many opportunities to represent and re-represent our developing thoughts and ideas (the 'hundred languages' of children);

3   having our learning 'scaffolded'.

Here is an example which might make you smile.

Five-year-old Chloe heard her five-month-old cousin babbling and wanted to know why he kept 'saying' the same sound over and over again. Her mother said that he wasn't yet able to talk but was trying to. Chloe then tried to get her 5-week-old brother to do the same by putting her face close to his and repeating the babbling sounds she had heard. To her delight the baby responded by making a random sound – a monosyllabic sound. She rushed off to tell her father that the baby was talking and that *he* had managed to say it only once.

In this example Chloe was bringing together what she had seen and heard, with what her mother had told her. In this way she was integrating her experiences. She then tried something out herself and arrived at a conclusion – an incorrect conclusion but one that is easy to understand and explain. This was an incident taking place at home with no one intending to teach Chloe anything. The feedback given in the form of an explanation from her mother was indirect.

Here are some examples set in a reception class. You decide which one is more likely to give the child feedback that will be useful in moving ahead.

▶   Example 1
The children have been given four pictures and have been asked to put them in the 'correct' order to match the story they have just heard. As the children work, the class teacher, working with one group, says to Mathilde, 'You are sitting so quietly and getting on with your work. Well done.'

The teacher's feedback in this example is about Mathilde's behaviour rather than about how well Mathilde has done with regard to the given task.

▶ Example 2
The teaching assistant, who is working with a different group on the same task, notices that Bruno has cut out the pictures very neatly but is having trouble putting them in order. She sits with him and says, 'What neat cutting out, Bruno. Can we sort these out together? Can you remember how the story started?'

The teaching assistant in this example watches carefully what the child is doing and comments on his physical skills – on his cutting. But she also asks him some questions which might stimulate him to be able to complete the given task.

▶ Example 3
At the end of the session the teacher comments favourably on some of the work done by the children but singles out Roman for special attention. She says to the class, 'I was so pleased with what Roman did. He spent a long time looking at the pictures before he started cutting them out and then he arranged them in order on a piece of paper and could then tell me a really good story from the way he had organised the pictures. It wasn't the same story that I read you, but it was a very good story anyway.'

The feedback from the teacher in this plenary session focuses clearly on the intellectual demands of the task, and her feedback to Roman, who had not re-told the story in the sequence expected by the teacher, nonetheless focused on what he *had* done and gave him credit for his work and his thinking.

All three adults gave positive feedback in the sense that they said something positive to each child. But which child do you think learned something from the feedback given? Do you think that telling Mathilde that she had sat quietly helped her to know what, in connection with the given task, she had done well? Bruno would certainly have benefited from having an adult sit with him and support him (scaffold his learning) as he worked out the sequence. But how about Roman? What was it that the teacher did that helped Roman in his learning?

My analysis of this incident leads me to feel that the teacher, paying close attention to what it was that Roman had done and remembering what the task had been for the children, managed to do several things:

▷ She gave some **positive feedback** saying how long Roman had stayed on task. In doing this she indicated to all the children that spending time doing something is worthwhile.

▷ She **outlined the process** he had gone through. This is scaffolding his learning because she is making him aware of the steps he took. Helping children develop their own awareness of their achievements is a crucial feature of good feedback.

▷ She managed to find the product (the end-result) worthwhile even though it had not met her original learning outcome – to put the pictures in the sequence of the story she had read to the children. In doing this she **showed the child that there was more than one way of solving the problem set**.

From this I would suggest that Roman knew he had worked hard, that he had produced something that was sequential and from which he could tell a story. He may also have realised that he had not done what was asked but, importantly, that that did not make his efforts worthless.

WHAT DO WE GIVE FEEDBACK ON?

You might want to think about what it is that you give feedback on. There is evidence to suggest that teachers in primary schools and nursery classes tend to give feedback against four main categories:

▷ The presentation or the neatness of the work. This is illustrated by comments like 'lovely writing', 'you copied the date neatly', 'no crossing out' and so on.

▷ The surface features of the work. This is illustrated by comments like 'Where is the full stop?' 'Copy out all the words you have spelled incorrectly' and so on.

▷ The amount of work. This is illustrated by comments like 'You have done a whole page of writing' or 'You coloured in the whole picture' or 'You have done 20 sums'.

▷ Effort. This is illustrated by comments like 'Well done. You tried hard'.

In the examples above you will remember that the children were praised for effort and also for positive behaviour. You will remember Mathilde being told that she had been 'sitting quietly'. Parents frequently complain that, when they go to open evenings to learn about how their children are getting on, they often get comments about the things listed above.

> Eve, parent of five-year-old Jamie, said, 'I know that he is a lovely little boy with dimples and that he is quiet and well behaved. I know that he can produce pages and pages of drawing or writing or whatever. I know he sometimes tries hard. What I want to know is how well is he doing. Is he getting better at making friends and being independent? Is he learning to read and write? Does he enjoy listening to stories in class? Is there anything he is particularly good at or interested in? Is there anything he is struggling with? These are the things I need teachers to tell me about.'

You will realise that the things we often comment on and give feedback about are the things that are easy to observe. One glance will indicate if a child is conforming and doing what was asked. One look at a piece of writing will tell the reader if it is neat and tidy or full of errors and crossing-out. The difficult thing is to give feedback that is focused and targeted.

In order to do that the adult has to think really carefully about what it was that the child was doing. In many classes you will be working with learning intentions or learning outcomes – what it is that children are expected to learn from a given activity. It is important to remember that with younger children, who are learning primarily through play, the learning intention will not be one given by the teacher but a more-difficult-to-identify one chosen by the child.

See if you can work out the learning intentions of the children in the following examples.

> Christopher, a bilingual 5-year-old living in Cyprus, wrote his name in Greek and English and proudly showed it to an adult. 'I can write in both languages', he said proudly.

The learning intention here is quite clear. Christopher set out to demonstrate something he knows he can do, which is to write his name in two languages, each with different scripts. The feedback given by the adult was something like 'You are amazing! I can't write my name in Greek and English', which enabled Christopher to respond, 'Well, I could teach you Greek. It's really easy!'

Manjit, playing with magnets, said that the silver balls were 'sticking' to the magnet. He then went round the room trying various other things to see if they would stick to the magnet. What do you think his learning intention was?

We cannot be certain, but it seems very likely that he was asking himself the question 'What things will stick to the magnet and what things will not?' His learning outcome was to find out which things would adhere to the magnet. The feedback given by the adult was 'What a lot of things you found that stick to the magnet. Do you know why these stick and other things don't?' Asking an open-ended question directly related to what the child had done allowed him the opportunity to start to make hypotheses about the properties of magnetism.

Maria, age 3, went into the book corner, sat on the floor and picked out a songbook. She then turned the pages, singing loudly to herself in Spanish, which is her first language.

Maria's learning intention might have been to look at some books. What feedback would you give to Maria? Would you tell her that the songbook contained English and not Spanish songs? Or would you consider that she is demonstrating that she knows that some books, with musical notes on the pages, have songs in them and is linking this to her own knowledge which is of Spanish songs? Might you be tempted to say something like 'You are clever to recognise that this is a song-book. It must be these [pointing to notes of music] that helped you know that.'

WHAT ABOUT REWARDS?

Many schools and even nurseries offer rewards for 'good work' or 'good behaviour': gold stars, smiley faces, weekly certificates, Star of the Week, Star of the Month, Star of the School, a points system and so on. In some places this is done sensitively and offers children opportunities to be noticed for many positive things and not merely for getting things right or 'being clever'.

Seven-year-old Anna, rewarded at a school assembly with comments about the fact that the teacher found it a pleasure to have her in the class, responded, 'Yeah, yeah! She says that every week about somebody.'

Children are very quickly able to sort out the undeserved and irrelevant praise from the praise that recognises individual and important things the child has said or done.

If you believe that learning should be the reward in itself then these extrinsic tokens of success are meaningless. For children who are following their own interests and doing things that are important to them (i.e. playing), just doing what they have set out to do is the reward. Here are some examples.

▶ Halya, building a complex structure with blocks, is delighted that the structure does not collapse. She claps her hands and calls the teacher over to admire her work.

▶ Rani, reading a book from beginning to end, is satisfied that the story was engrossing. She puts the book down with a sigh and goes out to play.

▶ Julie, drawing a picture of her baby brother to take home, has made something she wanted to make. When her mum comes to collect her she hands the picture to her baby brother who proceeds to chew it. Julie merely grins as her mother tells her what a silly baby he is.

▶ Greta and Gillian, writing the names of their friends in the register they have made, are happy to show it to all the children.

None of these children need gold stars or smiley faces to help them achieve. But a focused comment might help them become self-aware – to know what they can do.

Using the above examples let's look at the feedback given to the children.

▷ Halya's teacher, looking at the construction, comments that it is symmetrical. In doing this she not only shows Halya that she has been really taking notice of what it was that Halya was trying to do but also makes Halya know that she can build something symmetrical. She introduces Halya to a new word to describe what she has done.

▷ When the teacher comments to Rani that she had read a whole book in her head for the first time she helps Rani be aware of and confirm her own achievement.

▷ When the nursery nurse tells Julie that the picture of her baby brother looks just like him she helps Julie know that her picture is recognisable – despite her baby brother later destroying the picture!

▷ When, in the plenary session, the teacher asks Greta and Gillian to show the children the register they have made and points to the names they have spelled correctly she helps them both confirm what they already know and can do.

Becoming self-aware is a vital part of learning and targeted feedback is an essential tool in assisting children to do this.

SELF-AWARENESS AND SELF-ASSESSMENT

Knowing what you know and what you can do is important in deciding what you still need to know. If you are asked what you need to learn in order to be able to speak Italian on your next holiday you would have to stop and think about what, if any, Italian you already know. From eating Italian food you will know some words like 'espresso' or 'pizza', and from watching television you might know how to say hello to a friend or how to say thank you. A quick review of your existing knowledge is not difficult. You probably do this very often without even being conscious of what you are doing. Having done this, you are in a better position to identify what new vocabulary you want to acquire prior to your visit.

Small children are very able to reflect on what they have achieved, particularly where they are with adults who show a genuine interest in what they are doing.

Here are some examples of children reflecting on what they can do, sometimes in conversation and sometimes using what Vygotsky called 'inner speech', to give us, through these monologues, an insight into what they understand.

Josh, playing with cars on a ramp and talking, out loud, to himself. 'Down they go. Ooops! That one was REALLY fast. Again. It was fast again. I'll try this one. [Picks up a bigger car.] Even faster! I'll do two together. [Puts both cars at the top of the ramp.] The yellow one wins. That's because it is so fast!'

If you read this carefully you can see just how much Josh reveals, through this monologue, about the learning processes he is going through. He is actually describing each action he takes and telling us what he has noticed and what conclusions he has come to. In this example he has realised that the yellow car is the fastest.

Raza calls to the teacher, 'Elly, I need that thing. That sticking thing. The black one.'

In this example Raza reveals that he knows that he needs some help. He knows that he can ask for it and knows who to ask. He cannot remember the name of what he wants (the stapler) but can describe it.

Zohra comes home and tells her mum, 'I wrote a whole story in my book today'.

Zohra has recognised that writing a whole story is something worth telling her mum about. She is aware of her own achievement.

The skilled educator will try to provide opportunities for children to reflect on what they have learned and on what they already know and can do. This is often done by informal exchanges where the educator, interested in what the children have been doing, engages in conversation with them.

Here is an example of this:

The nursery nurse notices that a child has made a very complex model using many different resources. She sits down next to the child and starts a conversation.

'I love your model. You have used so many different things – egg boxes, toilet roll holders, lids and shiny things. Oh, and look, some buttons.'

The child, noticing that the adult is really interested and not just asking questions, joins in, saying 'It took me a long time, you know'. The adult responds, 'Yes, I noticed that you were busy doing it all morning, I wonder if that was because it was so difficult to fix some of the bits together.' The child replies, 'I used this strong glue and also some sellotape and Joshua [another child] gave me these . . . these . . . 'lastic bands and I used those.' The adult continues, 'Well, you have made a really exciting model with some bits that move. Are you going to take it home?'

You will notice that in this exchange the adult did not ask the child 'What did you make?' and the reason for this is that she was interested not in what the child made but in *how* the child made it. In other words, she was interested in the **process** of making something rather than in the object made. Getting an insight into what the child did helps the adult understand what problems the child encountered and how she solved them. This sensitive and astute nursery nurse has engaged in a genuine discussion with the *child* and in the process of really paying attention to what the child was paying attention to managed to help the child reflect on the process for herself. She also helped the child be aware of her own achievement.

In High Scope settings the staff introduce a system of self-reflection known as 'plan–do–review'. In this system children are asked to plan what they are going to do, then do it and then think back over what they have done. This thinking back or reflection is aimed at getting children to assess their own achievements. This method can work effectively when adults are sensitive to the fact that children's plans can change. It is important also to recognise that for some children – particularly younger children or those with little English – this can be a daunting experience and one in which they can become tongue-tied and silent.

Another common forum for self-reflection is in the 'plenary' session built into many lessons. Here, after the lesson or the session, the adult leads the group in a session where they reflect on what they have achieved, usually against a learning outcome. Plenary sessions are held in some reception classes and even in some nursery classes, but it is worth thinking carefully about how these are structured. Many young children find the formal format very daunting.

Teachers of older children sometimes draw up a list of the sorts of questions they might use to help children really think about what they have learned and achieved. Here are some drawn from a book by Shirley Clarke (2001):

▷   What did you find difficult while you were . . . ?
▷   What helped you when you got stuck? Was it a friend, the teacher, a book, your own thinking?
▷   What do you think you need more help with?
▷   What are you most pleased about?
▷   Have you learned anything new? What was it?
▷   Have you got any questions?

Here is how a very experienced reception class teacher used the plenary session at the end of the Literacy Hour.

'I watched everybody this morning and so did Maria [the teaching assistant] and we noticed so many wonderful things. Julian, can you show the children the picture you drew of the three owls on the branch and tell the children why you chose to draw on black paper?' (Julian shows the picture.) The teacher continues, 'What are you most pleased with about this picture?'

Julian replies, 'I like how I made them go from the biggest to the smallest on the branch.' The teacher thanks Julian and moves on to another child. 'Now Hameed did something wonderful this morning and I am sure he would like to tell you what he did.'

Hameed, very softly, 'I writed my name.' 'You did, Hameed, and it was perfect. Well done,' responds the teacher. 'And now last of all I want to ask the four children who were working with Maria what they learned this morning?'

Arvind says, 'We learned when you write a question you put a question mark.'

Sonya adds, 'And we wrote some questions the baby owls asked like "Where's my mummy?"'

You can see how sensitive questioning, based on careful and interested observation of what the children have been doing, helps young children come up with fascinating insights into their own learning. Here are some examples of comments collected from very young children reflecting on their own learning:

'When we were writing the register for our game we copied all the children's names from their trays.'

Here the child has indicated that they could not write all the names on their own. She has also shown that they have developed a strategy for dealing with this. They are well on the way to being independent learners.

'Miss, there aren't enough cups for the dolls. Can I go and get some from the other class?'

In play the child has noticed that there are not enough cups to give one to each doll . . . and again found a solution.

57

Two children building a wonderful tower explained how they had done it. When it came to the complex task of balancing one block on another at the top of the structure, one child explained to the adult, 'You need another person: someone to hold it while you balance the block on top.'

Again, an awareness of the complexity of the task and an understanding that it was something that could not be achieved alone.

Finally, a child in the reception class, just starting to write, wrote a message to the teacher which he 'read' back: 'I like writing but I can't do it so my mum can read it.'

You decide what this child has understood about his own learning. In this chapter we have explored the importance of careful, sensitive and targeted feedback and seen how even very young children can be helped to start reflecting on what they have been doing, what they have enjoyed and what they may have struggled with.

Cathy Nutbrown writes: 'To extend learning opportunities, to challenge children to think, to question, to discover and to evaluate their learning, teachers must work interactively in partnership with children' (1994: 149). She reminds us that teachers need to be involved in the activities alongside children so that they can give proper feedback on what is happening. She uses a phrase you might find helpful: 'For children to learn effectively their teachers must "feed back" to them in order that there can be a "feed forward" in learning' (ibid.: 149).

SUMMING UP

In this chapter we have looked at how we can use what we have noticed about children through observing their play or looking at their work in order to help them take the next step in learning. In doing this we have thought about the importance of giving feedback that will make sense to the child and allow the child to recognise both what has been achieved and what needs to be improved. Giving feedback and marking or making comments on work or behaviour is an essential part of the learning process.

GLOSSARY

Conscious	When we talk of someone being conscious of something we mean that they are aware of it.
Extrinsic tokens of success	Extrinsic means outside, and this phrase describes things like stars and other rewards given to children for doing well. Intrinsic rewards would be the rewards that come from the pleasure of knowing you have done something well.
Feedback	The process whereby something that happens has an effect on what happens next. In education, feedback is when someone helps the learner know what has been achieved and this helps the learner take the next step.
Higher-order thinking	This is a phrase used by psychologists and others who consider learning, and it applies to things like problem-solving or thinking abstractly – i.e. without props.
Inner speech	This was a phrase used by Vygotsky. He believed that inner speech came before thought. Young children often speak their thoughts aloud: when this stops it appears that thinking becomes internal. This is inner speech.
Plenary	This is when students and educators review what has happened and try to see if the learning outcomes have been met. During the Literacy Hour, for example, the last section of the lesson is set aside as a plenary.
Positive feedback	This is where the educator tells the learner some of the good things the learner has done. It is similar to praise although it is more focused.

Process	In this context the process is what the child does, often on the way to making the product. So the process is the physical act of drawing or building or writing of the products described above.
Product	In this context product refers to what the child makes. So the product can be a picture or a construction or a piece of writing.
Symmetrical	A mathematical term used to describe something that is the same on both sides of a mid-line.

Chapter 5

Learning and assessment

A workshop for you

✔ In this chapter you will be invited to read some examples of children at work and at play in classrooms and other places. You will then be asked to practise your skills of assessment by suggesting what it is these children know and can do.

✔ You will then be asked to think about what you might set up in your workplace to support these children (if they were in your group) so that their learning and development can be extended.

✔ You will then be invited to reflect on what you have learned from doing this.

The format of this chapter is slightly different in that it is made up of a number of case studies which you are invited to read and reflect on.

CASE STUDY 1: PLAYING AT HOME

It is a hot, sunny day. Two children (we will call them Anna and Sam) are playing out in the garden. The adult with them has taped some sheets of paper to the wall, mixed some paints and offered them brushes and palettes for mixing colours. Both children get excited at the paper on the wall and start painting, but quickly lose interest and the paints are left to dry in the sun. The adult with them is interested in this and also eager to find something that will happily occupy them both. She has no interest in 'teaching' them anything.

She notices that they are pottering on the edges of the small pond in the garden and thinks they might like their own bowl of water and some pouring things to play with. The children fill and empty some of the containers, but quickly lose interest. The adult then fetches a tub of Lego and suggests to one of the children, Sam, that he might like to build some boats. Anna immediately shows interest in doing the same thing and the two set about using the small Lego blocks and Lego people to construct a series of boats.

At first they make simple boats, each with one Lego person on them. They make them, try them out in the bowl of water to 'check that they float' and then float them 'for real' in the pond. The boats become more and more complex and both children are intensely involved in working collaboratively to design and test out the boats. When something sinks or falls over they discuss, eagerly, what the cause might be. They take the boat back to their 'trial tank' as they make modifications and the boat is only returned to the pond once they have sorted out the problem. It is Anna's idea to use the plastic bowl as what she calls a 'trial tank'.

At one point they stop working to go inside for a discussion about how to make the boats move more effectively. Sam considers attaching an elastic band around the propeller he has attached to one of the boats. Anna makes a boat with an attachment which she describes as an 'oar'. They both use a large plastic spoon to create 'whirlpools and currents' to speed the movement of the boats in the pond.

Still later they decide to name each of the people and the people are named after themselves and their friends. The game moves on so that there is only one person on each boat and a race is held to see who the winner is. From this the people are paired and another race is held to see who the winners are.

The children stop for lunch and for snacks. They stop to go inside and watch something on the television. They have a pause for an argument. But the play is sustained for over five hours and, indeed, in the case of Sam, carries on into the next day.

I wonder if you can make a guess at the ages of these two children. Did you think that they were the same age? In fact Anna is 7 and Sam is 5. In their play they were able to bring their own individual strengths and interests together so that they were genuinely collaborating on a joint venture which was of interest to both. Anyone who tells you that young children have a limited concentration span should think about this example. Here, with no teaching agenda, no National Curriculum, no learning goals and no worksheets, two young children worked incredibly hard at solving a whole set of problems they had created for themselves.

This is an example of real, deeply involving play. What interests me is how much the observer (or, in this case, the reader) can learn about each of the children through this prolonged play sequence.

Let me tell you more to help contextualise the observation for you. The children are siblings. Anna is in Year 2 and is an avid reader, with a wide general knowledge drawn from her reading and a powerful imagination. She has been making stories from when she was very young. Storying is probably her favourite way of making sense of her experiences. Sam is coming to the end of his first year of formal schooling. He has been a constructor and a problem-solver for as long as anyone can remember. He plans carefully, often vocalises what he is doing and has developed a very personal style of exploration, trial and error and the reaching of conclusions. If you had to find ways of describing the two children's learning styles you might characterise Anna as being a 'narrator' and Sam as being an 'investigator', although it is clear that both children use different strategies in all the situations in which they play and learn.

Imagine now that these two children had demonstrated all that was seen in the observation within your classroom or setting. Don't worry about their ages, but think about what you have learned about what these children already know and about what they can already do.

Here is my summary. Read it through to see if it agrees with yours.

▷ Sam can try things out. He can explain what he is doing. He takes notice of what happens and, if necessary, makes changes to what he is doing in response to this. He can concentrate for very long periods of time. He can collaborate.

▷ Anna can try things out. She can explain what she is doing. She takes notice of what happens and, if necessary, makes changes to what she is doing in response to this. She can concentrate for very long periods of time. She can collaborate.

You will see that I have said the same things about both children. I can add some other things that will help you see both the similarities and the differences between them.

Sam was often the leader in terms of the planning of the boats, although he needed Anna's greater physical dexterity to help him. Anna was the leader in terms of planning the games. It was her idea to personalise the game by giving the people names and by having races.

Having thought about what the children know and can do, you might now want to think about what activities you might plan for these children, or for children like them, to take their learning forward. I put this scenario to a group of students and childcare workers and asked them what they would offer, with what learning objectives in mind. Here are some of the ideas they came up with.

Imad: I would want to extend this by offering them different materials to use to make boats. I thought of bits of wood. I think they would be interested in exploring different ways of making boats.

Sheila: I don't think you have evidence that they are interested in making boats. I think they are interested in floating and sinking and I would link this to the curriculum and give them things to group according to whether they float or sink.

Imad: I suppose you would give them a worksheet to complete, then.

Sheila: I might. At least then I would have a record of if they know what floats and sinks.

Lesley: Stop arguing, you two. Anyway, I think you are both wrong. I think they might be interested in doing the whole thing on a different scale. I was thinking about giving them Duplo blocks instead of Lego and then seeing what happens.

Debbie: That's quite a good idea. I was thinking about getting them to predict which person on which boat would go fastest and then checking it out and perhaps recording their findings in some way on paper.

Michael: I like that. If you did that they could continue to work together. I loved the fact that they collaborated and so perhaps my focus would be on their social and emotional development.

The discussion went on for quite a while and many alternatives and ideas were discussed. I wonder what you felt and what your plans were.

Here is another case study and one that might be familiar to you.

CASE STUDY 2: CHRISTOPHER HAS A BABY BROTHER

Four-year-old Christopher has just gained a baby brother. He was very settled in the nursery until about two weeks ago when he started throwing the dolls on the floor, hitting them and refusing to do anything he was asked to do. It was clear to everyone in the nursery that he was very jealous of the baby, scared of showing his real feelings at home, so trying to vent his anger on the dolls in the safe environment of the nursery. The staff happily read him stories about new babies and tried to talk to him. But when he decided to turn his anger on other children, the nursery staff had a meeting to decide what to do. Since other children were getting hurt and parents were beginning to complain, they clearly had to do more than what their instincts told them to do – which was to give him time to deal with his feelings safely.

They had a meeting and the headteacher brought with her to the meeting a copy of a checklist designed by the educator Lilian Katz together with her colleague Diane McLellan. This 'Young Children's Social Development Checklist' requires those working with the children to carefully observe the child and monitor interactions between children over a period of time. They recommend that this be done every three or four months. The aim of the checklist is to observe the child to see what the child usually does and to understand variations in this 'normal' behaviour in light of how best to help the child. Some of the items on the checklist might interest you.

The child usually:

1   approaches others positively;
2   expresses wishes and preferences clearly and gives reasons for actions and positions;
3   asserts own rights and needs appropriately;
4   expresses anger and frustration effectively and without harming others or property;
5   gains access to ongoing groups at play and work;
6   does not draw inappropriate attention to self.

And so on.

The staff agreed that Christopher was, usually, socially skilled and that there were only one or two items on the list giving cause for concern – primarily item 4. In his play, Christopher was expressing his anger and frustration through harming others. One of the members of staff felt that this could be dealt with by talking to Christopher about what was happening. Two days later the same member of staff took the little boy aside after he had hurt someone during play and spoke to him very firmly, but making clear that it was his behaviour that was unacceptable and that everyone in the nursery still liked him and wanted him to be happy. The staff also spoke to Christopher's mum, who decided she would talk to him and try to let him express anger at home. It took about a month for Christopher's anger at the nursery to stop affecting the other children, although he still occasionally threw things and had tantrums.

CASE STUDY 3: PIERRE SETS THE TABLE

Here is another case study, this time drawn from the work of one of Piaget's associates, Greco (1962).

Greco tells the tale of 5-year-old Pierre, living with his family in Paris. Pierre could count to thirty and his mother decided it was time to involve him in the routines of daily life. Every day he was asked to put out the table napkins for the four members of the family.

On the first day he only took out one napkin, which he put on a plate. He then looked at what he had done, returned to the cupboard and took out a second napkin. He repeated this process until he had four napkins on four plates. Nobody commented on what he had done. Three months later he suddenly decided to count four plates and then four napkins and he distributed these around the table. He repeated this procedure for six days, but on the seventh day there was a guest for dinner and one more plate provided by Pierre's mother. Pierre repeated his daily routine of four plates and four napkins in four places and then noticed the spare plate.

What do you think he did? The logical thing might have been to return to the cupboard to collect an additional napkin. This is not what Pierre did, however. He returned all the napkins to the cupboard and began all over again, this time making five trips.

The next day there was no guest and Pierre returned to making four trips and continued in this way for five more days. At that time he seemed to re-discover his counting method. After ten days of counting accurately he was told that a guest was coming. This time he distributed his four napkins in the usual way and went to get a fifth napkin when he noticed the empty plate. The next day, when there was no guest present, he counted the number of plates before fetching the napkins, and after that no number of guests caused him any difficulties.

What do you make of this example? Do you see Pierre as a foolish child? Do you see his mother as foolish for not telling him how to do this more efficiently? If she had told him to count the plates and the napkins he would, undoubtedly, have learned to follow her orders and would have set the table efficiently, but without any thinking or reasoning of his own. He would have learned to follow a recipe and this is often what children are asked to do in schools. You will need to think carefully about how you want to foster children's learning and development and you might decide, like Pierre's mother, to let children think and invent their own solutions to problems.

CASE STUDY 4: YIAN READS HIS BOOK

Yian is 5 and in the reception class of his local school. He is a bright little boy who loves doing anything physical. His mother comments that when he comes out of school at the end of the day he is like a wound-up toy. He has to run and jump all the way home and when he gets indoors he charges about the house for about ten minutes before he collapses in a heap in front of the television. He likes books and stories and using the computer. He loves building and playing with cars and riding his bike. At school he seems happy enough. He has friends and seems to enjoy most aspects of school life – apart from school dinners, which he says he 'hates'! All year the class has been doing 'sound of the week' and in this way Yian has learned the names of the letters of the alphabet and the sounds they make. Once a week he brings home a book in his book bag and he is expected to 'read' this book aloud to his mum or dad and get it signed off in the little booklet, which goes around in his book bag.

Both parents find the books he brings home boring. They don't say this to Yian, of course, but they are aware that he cannot find in them what he finds so pleasurable in his home books – a story where things happen and his attention is held. In fact, in the last few months, he has been listening to stories in 'chapter books' and he loves the moment when the chapter ends and he is left wondering what might happen next. Suspense and prediction are familiar to him from television programmes too, but they are completely lacking in the simple primers he brings home from school.

His mother – who is a teacher – has started to worry about what happens when he tries to read the books he brings home. She comments,

> 'When he gets stuck on a word – which is almost all the time because he is so busy trying to sound out each word – he just keeps looking at me with panic in his eyes. It is obvious to me that he has lost track of the meaning of what he is reading and his eyes don't move ahead as they do when I read to him. It seems essential to me for him to stay with the meaning otherwise he just "barks at print".'

When probed about how she handled this she went on to say,

> 'Mostly I just abandon all attempts to get him to read and read to him. I invite him to laugh at the funny bits – if there are any – or to guess what might happen next, because that keeps him thinking ahead. I worry that he is beginning to feel like a failure and there is nothing like feeling like a failure to become a failure.'

How would you interpret Yian's reading behaviour when you think about what you have read about him? Would you agree with his mother's diagnosis and with her way of dealing with him?

Here are some other things you might like to know about Yian to get a fuller picture of his development:

▷ He loves 'the letter of the week' and fervently makes lists every week of the words he can think of that start with the letter.

▷ He uses everything he knows about sounds and letters to write the words on his lists. Here are some of the words he wrote for the letter Y – the start of his name:

    YLO   YAIN   YGT   YONI

(Can you work them out? They say: yellow, Yian, yoghurt and Yoni (the name of his friend.))

▷ He has two older brothers and both are quick learners, read fluently and with passion and enjoy reading stories to him.

▷ He is learning to play the piano and can do different things with each hand at the same time.

He is clearly a very able child growing up in a home where there are many opportunities for learning and many people around to help him. If you were his teacher and his mother had been to see you to share her concerns about his reading, what advice would you give her?

68

This is what happened. The teacher listened carefully to Yian's mother and matched what she heard to her own observation that Yian was becoming less and less keen to take books home. Because she was prepared to listen to a parent she learned from the exchange, and both agreed that Yian should stop taking home primers and should, instead, borrow story books and that the staff should write in the reading record that this was a book for the parents or brothers to read aloud and for Yian to comment on.

So once a week Yian's parents recorded the things Yian said. Here are some examples:

▶ This was a funny story.
▶ I liked where the bear fell in the lake.
▶ This book made me scared.

When Yian transferred to Year 1 he was not yet reading, but within a couple of months, freed from the pressure and no longer feeling as though he might fail, he began to take home books like the other children. Yian is now 8 years old and a fluent reader.

CASE STUDY 5: 'I CAN SING A RAINBOW'
(taken from a chapter by Roger Hancock with Alison Cox (2003))

In this chapter the author describes what happens when a group of children under the age of 3 visit a workshop at Tate Britain in London. Children and parents arrive at the workshop. Some have been before but none of the parents know each other and they stay close to their children. The room is set up with much to look at and the children join in with some singing and with some music and movement using scarves and fabric. The staff explain what will happen when they go into the galleries. A painting is selected and the children and parents sit on the floor in front of it while a staff member draws attention to the circles in the painting. Children are then invited to produce their own circles on brightly coloured paper. Children and adults work together – talking, cutting, tearing and sticking circles onto paper. After a while the group moves on. This time they stand, close together, in front of the famous Matisse painting 'The Snail'. The staff member invites them to trace the pattern, moving a finger 'anti-clockwise'. The adults do it and the children watch or imitate. The morning moves on following this pattern of sitting or standing in front of one particular painting and then joining in with what is asked. After an hour they return to the home base for drinks and biscuits. The staff have laid out art materials and children and adults enjoy mixing paints and making patterns and shapes. It is true play with materials. The morning ends with a song.

Do you regard this as a worthwhile thing for children and their parents or carers to do? What do you think such very young children learned from this? Are there things in this that you could offer within your setting to encourage physical development, creative development, personal and social development?

SUMMING UP

In this chapter you have been offered a series of case studies to read and think about. You might ask 'What has this to do with assessment?' and I hope that you can answer this question for yourself. We cannot know what children can do unless we watch them, listen to them and take them seriously. When we know what they can do, we can think about what *we* can do to help them take another step in learning. Then we have to watch them and listen to them again to see what they now know. So we observe, assess, plan, and start all over again. In our planning, which is based on what we have observed, we have to build in a degree of challenge to ensure that children move ahead in their learning.

And what about the children? In the best practice they choose what to do, they get very involved in doing what they have chosen and face up to the challenges encountered. At the end they are tired, but satisfied. That is learning (and play) at its best.

Chapter 6

Who are the experts?

✔ In this chapter we regard the children as experts on their own learning and consider how we can give them opportunities to do this.

✔ We also think about the expertise offered by the nursery nurse, the teaching assistant, the special needs support assistants and others.

✔ And we come to the particular knowledge and expertise held by the parents, carers and others in the community.

If you were asked who the experts are in terms of knowing about and assessing children's learning, development and progress you would almost certainly think, first, of the class teacher. It is true, of course, that the class teacher – who has learned something about 'child development' – will be able to say how well a child is doing relative to other children in the class or to how well the child was doing six months ago. But it is important to consider that there are others who can be regarded as 'experts' and these include the children themselves.

EXPERT CHILDREN: CHILDREN ASSESSING THEIR OWN LEARNING

You might question this assertion, thinking that very young children do not have the intellectual competence to assess their own progress and development, and it is true, of course, that children's understanding of what they know and can do is related to their age and to their maturity.

But we do have a tendency to dismiss young children as being not yet cognitively competent when often they are. Our views of children's competence in this area come from a very narrow and Western view of what competence is. If you think about the lives of children in the countries you may have visited on holiday, seen on television or read about in books, you will realise that many children are involved in doing things as part of their normal lives that we would regard as unaccept-able within developed Western societies. Take, for instance, the example that appears in Rogoff (1990) of a baby of 11 months photographed cutting a fruit with a machete. This appears to many here as shocking and dangerous and yet the reality is that, for many of the world's chil-dren, being part of the world of work is what life is about. The AIDS pandemic in sub-Saharan Africa has left many young children as the heads of families. Street children in many African cities engage in complex transactions as they earn money to survive. This must make us think about how narrow our views of children and of their capacities are. No one would want our children to have to deal with the diffi-culties these children have to deal with. But what we do need to think about is how we can consult children about their own feelings about what they are doing. We need to hear their voices and attend to what they say.

Lansdown (1996) reminds us that article 12 of the United Nations Convention on the Rights of the Child states that all children have the right to express their own views on anything that affects them and to have their views taken seriously. This applies not only to their family lives but also to anything that concerns their health, their education and their development. Educators have, traditionally, paid scant attention to this, particularly educators of young children. Often children are viewed as being in need of adult care and protection and advice, and children *are*, at times, in need of these things. Evidence of the lives of children in less developed countries shows just how capable, competent and thoughtful young children have to be and how seriously they need to be taken.

Some schools, taking the issue of children's rights seriously, have set up mechanisms for ensuring that children have some voice in the life of the school. This varies from very crude to relatively successful, where schools have school councils and peer mediators and mentors and so on. In some schools only children aged 7 and above are involved in these councils, while in others even children in the reception class are involved. Much depends on how these things are set up, but what children say about them is revealing.

> 5-year-old Rowan said: 'I was smashed into the wall and I didn't do anything. I was just watching my friends and they were the ones being naughty. I was sent to Miss S's office and I had to stand there all afternoon and that was very unfair. I didn't tell Miss S who did it, but afterwards I went and found the peer mediator and told her and she told Miss S. And then I thought Miss S should say sorry to me but she didn't.'

Rowan's description of what happened is revealing. He explains the events but also makes a judgement about how he was treated, using the word 'unfair' which indicates a developing sense of justice. He didn't 'tell on' his friends, but found an extremely mature way of dealing with the situation by seeking out the peer mediator. His comment that the headteacher should have apologised to him, but didn't, shows how much he has internalised about what he is expected to do when he makes a mistake and how he generalises this to adults. He is learning something important about how rules for adults and children, or strong and weak, vary.

> 4-year-old Amina came home very upset and told her mum she wasn't going back to nursery. It took a lot of gentle probing to find out what had happened but in the end Amina revealed the fact that two other little girls kept holding their noses when they sat next to her.

In this example Amina, thinking back over what had happened to her, recognised that something unfair had taken place. There are either no structures for helping her deal with this in her nursery or she is not aware of them. But in her account she can articulate what is upsetting her.

In terms of learning there are many excellent examples of inviting children to assess their own achievements. In settings where this takes place, staff are clear that where children are in charge of what they are doing (i.e. their play) they can also evaluate what they have done. Children invited to do this are not dependent on adult evaluations and can make judgements about their own successes, and this is a crucial life skill. Fisher (1999) tells us that there are particular questions which teachers use to prompt children to reflect on their own learning:

▷ What interests the child?
▷ What the child enjoys?
▷ What the child wants to do?
▷ What help the child needs in order to learn or do?
▷ What the child would like to know?

73

Dan has developed an interest in paper aeroplanes. The teacher has noticed this and is aware of what his interests are. In response he has provided the child with lots of pieces of paper of different sizes and weights. Dan spends the morning using different sizes of paper to make planes. He cuts and he folds and he flies them. At the end of the morning the teacher invites him to tell the other children what he has been doing. He holds up one example after another and, prompted by the teacher, tells the children which size of paper worked best. The teacher asks questions like:

What makes you think this paper is best?

How did you test the aeroplanes?

What are you going to do next?

What did you learn this morning?

His answer to the last question is revealing:

'Light paper is good but some heavy paper is also good. I think I need to know how to make a different shaped plane. I've got one at home that is made of wood and that flies really well.'

Can you see how he has really thought about what worked and why and he has been able to link his school experience to home and plan what he might do next? Impressive thinking for a 5-year-old!

EXPERT ADULTS: PLANNING FOR SELF-REFLECTION

Good practitioners think about how their planning will allow children – even very young children – time and opportunities to think about their own learning. Here is an example of the planning and reviewing process in one very large High Scope open-plan primary school.

The children in 'red class' are in the Foundation Stage, in the reception class. At the start of the session the children go into their room, sit on the carpet and look at books while their names are called on the register. The teaching assistant then hands out their weekly planning books and invites them to find the page for that day. She helps any children who are struggling. The children then either write what they want to do, draw a picture of what they want to do or find the relevant sticker. The stickers say things like:

Making something with found materials;

Playing in the sand;

Listening to a story;

Doing some reading;

Building with the blocks;

Playing in the home corner.

A picture accompanies each simple statement.

The teacher, the teaching assistant and the language support assistant, Priya, then choose three children each to talk to about their plans and to check on at the end of the session. This follows a carefully constructed programme ensuring that every child is tracked regularly. They are the adult experts who are planning time to help the children reflect on their own learning.

This conversation was overheard between the language support assistant and 6-year-old Keira.

Priya: Oh Keira, I can see that you are going to make something in the making area today. Have you got any idea what you want to make?
Keira shakes her head.

Priya: Shall we go over there and have a look at what things there are. That might give you some idea.
They go to the creative area and together explore the materials on the table and in containers clearly accessible to the children. Keira selects some shiny card; some lengths of paper; some sequins in a tab; and two toilet roll holders.

Keira: I'm going to use these.

Priya: They look lovely. Is there anything else you need? Think about sticking the bits together.

Keira: I will need glue – that strong kind – and maybe some of those clip things.

Priya: I will get you the glue while you find a place to work. Perhaps you want to draw your ideas before you start.
Keira shakes her head, goes off and finds a place at the table and starts to explore the materials. When Priya returns Keira is hard at work. Priya makes some notes in her observation notebook and then goes off to find her second target child.

75

At the end of the morning Priya returns to find Keira and to talk to her about her finished work.

Priya: Are you happy with what you made?

Keira: It is a room for my Barbie doll.

She shows Priya what she has made and Priya is surprised to see that the shiny card has not been used and has been replaced by a shoebox and in the shoebox are lots of sequins, curly pieces of paper, bits of fabric and some tiny boxes.

Priya: Will you tell the children at 'show' time what you made?

Keira agrees. This is what she says.

Keira: I was going to make something shiny but then I saw Tahiba using a box and I got one too and then I stuck the sequins on the walls and put this stuff on the floor for a carpet and then I found some little boxes and used them for the cupboards. Tahiba helped me cut some of the things because it was hard and she is bigger than me. It isn't finished yet. I am going to make a bed tomorrow.

Can you see how the adult helped the child take control of her learning and reflect on what she had done, what she had achieved and what she still wanted to do? Here are the notes Priya wrote in the child's profile:

Wednesday 5th May: K chose the creative area. She had a plan based around shiny resources but later changed her plan and made a room for her Barbie doll. She was influenced by an older child and asked that child for help, recognising her greater skill at cutting. She was able to describe what she had done, the problems she encountered, the solution she found and she was able to plan ahead.

Priya has a specific role in this class. She works particularly with the children who have English as an additional language. Keira came to England a year ago with no English and she has learned efficiently and effectively as she plays and learns alongside her peers. The school does not believe in isolating second-language learners, but feels strongly that they learn mostly through being involved in things that interest them and where the meaning is embedded in the task. Priya will, however, invite Keira and some of the other EAL learners to come to her story session where she will use a story with repetition built into the text, or use story props or puppets, or do some singing and role-play. Whatever she does will be aimed at helping the children get at the meaning and become involved in understanding the story or the songs.

Priya and the teaching assistant both play a role in observing children, assessing their learning and contributing to the records kept by the class teacher. They each play the role of 'key worker', taking special responsibility for overseeing the progress of nine children. The teacher takes responsibility for the remaining twelve and is ultimately responsible for checking the profiles of each child to make sure that they are up to date, cover the whole curriculum and are written in a style that is meaningful to the parents who will read them.

EXPERT ADULTS: PARENTS UNDERSTANDING LEARNING

We often hear people talk about how parents are experts about their own children. This is, of course, true. Parents know their children better than anyone else and see their children in contexts which are not available to teachers or nursery nurses. Many parents may know a great deal about children learning but there will always be some parents who find their children's behaviour difficult to understand and respond to. This is often the case with behaviours that appear to be very repetitive and seemingly meaningless. To make this clear, here is an example:

Two-year-old Imran irritates his mother by taking things from one place to another. He takes his clean clothes and puts them in the doll's pram, wheels them to his mum's bed, takes them out and puts them on the bed. Ten minutes later he wheels them back to his room and unpacks them. He transports things from one place to another.

This seemingly random behaviour is, in fact, recognised by educators as an important part of learning and development. Chris Athey (1990) pointed out that children – particularly between the ages of 2 and 5 – engage in repeated patterns of behaviour in their attempts to draw on their previous experience in order to make sense of new experiences. Drawing on the language of Piaget, these repeated patterns are called schemas. Theorists like Athey have described and defined a whole set of these schemas and you will recognise some of them. The vertical schema, for example, is where a child is exploring the impact of up and down movements. You can see evidence of schemas in children's mark making and in their exploratory play. Other defined schemas include enveloping, rotation, going over and under, and so on.

The importance of this is to be aware of the importance of repeated patterns of behaviour and to discuss these with parents so that they can both look out for them and recognise that they are not random and useless, but, on the contrary, essential to learning and development. Many nurseries offer parents a workshop or a booklet in which schemas are described and discussed. Here are some excerpts from a handbook for parents all about schemas:

> We know that the word 'schema' is a bit off-putting, but understanding what it means can help you understand more about your own child. The word comes from the work of Piaget who saw children's learning as a process from action to thought. The child tries things over and over again to work out things like 'What things are suckable' and then works out categories of suckable and non-suckable things. So the child knows that dummies and thumbs are suckable but stones and leaves aren't. Here are some of the common repeated patterns of behaviour. We include these to help you recognise what your child is doing and try and work out what questions he or she is asking.
>
> *Enclosure:* Your child might like to put boundaries round things. Maybe he or she puts fences round the farm animals, puts the doll in the cradle or the pram, or puts lines around the end of the paper. What your child is exploring is things like the meaning of inside and outside, full and empty, space and boundaries.
>
> *Transporting:* Your child might drive you mad by taking things from one place to another. He or she might carry the toys from one part of the flat to another. He or she might fill up bags and baskets and trolleys and then empty them out again. We think your child might be exploring things like space and movement and distance and how to convey different things and so on.

You can see how the parents in this setting are being informed about some theoretical aspects of learning in an attempt to help them understand what might seem like strange behaviour in their children. Treating the parents respectfully like this is part of setting up meaningful partnerships.

The close involvement of parents in any setting for young children is very important. In the United Kingdom, the Code of Practice, the Sure Start guidance and the Curriculum Guidance highlight the importance of such partnerships for the successful learning and development of children. Internationally there is a long history of acknowledging the importance of such partnerships and there has been some research in the United States which found that high levels of parental involvement were a key factor in what were described as successful early years programmes (Perry Preschool High Scope Project in Schweinhart *et al.* 1993).

There is, however, a danger in this, and that is the danger of assuming that there is only one way of being a 'good' parent and that is a very Western, white and middle-class way. Good parents are expected to attend open evenings, to be able to read with their children at home, to support the setting or school in every way. The reality is that many parents are not able to do these things because of the pressures of their lives. Other parents may choose not to, thinking of teachers and educators as the experts and being unwilling to reveal what might be seen as their own inadequacies. So while parental partnerships may be desirable, it is important that educators are sensitive and aware of differences in expectations and experiences.

There are some fine examples of partnerships coming from the nurseries of Reggio Emilia. There the nurseries are regarded as a resource for the whole community and not only parents but workers, politicians, artists and researchers are all involved in the partnerships. The education of the children is seen as the responsibility of the whole community and the view is that the children represent the future of the community and must, therefore, receive the best possible education. It is important to add that the circumstances of these nurseries are different from many in this country because the communities are far more homogeneous than many here.

Research cited by Butt and Box (1998) indicates that black and other ethnic-minority parents are very reluctant to attend the currently popular parenting classes or to visit family centres. There is no doubt that many of these parents might indeed benefit from advice or support – as other parents may do – but something about the ways in which these classes or centres are set up is alien to them. Some interesting research from the USA describes a programme called *Strengthening Families: Strengthening Communities* (Steele *et al.* 2000). Although this programme has much in common with other models of parental involvement it has some distinct and perhaps unique features. The most interesting is that it explicitly values the cultural history of the families and examines ways in which parents can be helped to pass this on to their children. This is a positive model and one that does not focus on problems.

In England an example of close professional contact comes from the Thomas Coram Early Excellence Centre which is situated in a richly diverse community in central London. The focus of their partnership programme is the learning of the children. The partnership process involves operating a key worker system, having a long settling-in period, having in-depth conferences with parents about the child, ensuring that parents are kept informed about daily events, and organising regular times when parent and key worker can meet to review the child's progress. At these meetings the parent and key worker talk not only about the child's progress but also decide on priorities for the child's future learning and development and work out ways in which they can work together on this.

The staff at the centre recognise that parents are often working or studying and they continue to explore different ways of ensuring that all parents have access to information from the centre and a way of expressing their own views. These include the following:

▷ books which go from home to centre, in which key worker and parent record their views and thoughts;
▷ regular newsletters and information sheets;
▷ a website;
▷ invitations to parents to join particular projects.

The centre employs a training coordinator who runs a group for staff members who wish to improve their skills as trainers, and this involves them being observed as they work with parents in groups. Draper and Duffy (2001) cite the example of one group which is meeting to discuss 'Why does my child do that?' – which takes us back to the example of Imran and others like him.

EXPERT EXPERTS: WHO ELSE CAN BE INVOLVED?

Where you, or a parent, have serious concerns about some aspect of a child's development, you are able to seek the expert advice of a range of professionals. The experts involved assess the children they see and communicate their findings to the school or setting. Such experts might include:

▷ speech and language therapists, who have a particular expertise in the acquisition and development of language;

▷ educational psychologists, who focus on the cognitive development of children; clinical psychologists, who focus on children's personal, social and emotional behaviour;

▷ occupational therapists, who can advise on particular aids for children with specific difficulties;

▷ doctors, paediatricians, nurses and other health professionals, who all have a role to play where there are questions about health.

Your school or setting will be able to let you know which expert to turn to for problems you encounter. It is important for practitioners to establish professional relationships with these experts and to communicate as partners about the development of the child.

GLOSSARY

Conference with parents	Where a teacher or key worker spends time talking to a parent about the child's learning and development.
EAL	This stands for English as an Additional Language and is the accepted way of describing children who speak languages other than English or in addition to English.
Found materials	Often found in the area of the setting known as the creative or making area and referring to things like toilet rolls, egg boxes and other resources that have been collected together.
Foundation Stage	The first stage of formal education in England which applies to children from the age of 3 until the age of 6. It refers to the curriculum in all settings.
High Scope	An American-based early years curriculum based on children planning, doing and reviewing what they have done.
Key worker	Many settings operate this system where each child has one particular adult who is

	the key person in relating to the child and overseeing the child's learning and development.
Language support teacher	A teacher who has the particular role of supporting children's language development. This teacher may be assigned primarily to children with EAL but in many settings the language support teacher will be a resource for developing the language of all children.
Mediator	Someone who intervenes where there is disagreement and tries to get the parties involved to sort things out.
Open plan	An area designed with few walls and often divided up into different areas.
Profile	The place where observations and assessments are gathered together to give a picture of each child's development and learning.
Schema	A term used by Piaget to describe repeated patterns of behaviour.
School council	A body set up in some schools and settings to ensure that children can have a voice in discussing what is happening to them.
Settling-in period	Phrase used to describe the time it takes for children to adjust to new classes or groups.
Story props	Things used to enable children to grasp the meaning of a story and recreate it for themselves. Can include cut-outs, magnetic figures, puppets, etc.
Story with repetition	Many stories are written to include repeated phrases. An example is 'Run, run as fast as you can. You can't catch me. I'm the Gingerbread Man.'

Chapter 7

Record-keeping, profiling and conferencing

✔ In this chapter we consider ways in which parents can be invited to share their views about their children's progress as part of building up a profile of their development.

✔ We look at ways for children to contribute to the profile.

✔ We examine the sorts of things that might be put into a profile.

✔ We look at why we keep records, how to manage them and some of the principles underlying them.

Note: The term 'profile' is used to describe ways of gathering together the work of individual children but it is also used, in England, to describe a specific requirement for teachers working with children at the end of the Foundation Stage. In this chapter we are considering the first definition.

SOME REMINDERS: SIGNIFICANT MOMENTS AND CONFERENCING

Wherever you are working you are going to be involved in several aspects of assessment. You will — by the very nature of the work that you do — be observing children and taking notice of what they say and do. You will probably have a system in place whereby you write down your observations and use these as the basis for deciding what each child you have observed needs to do next. If you are fortunate enough to be in a well-organised setting you will also be involved in building up profiles of children's work.

A profile is a collection of things related to an individual child which, taken together, give a detailed account of the child's progress and development. These include work done by the child, work observed by adults, comments made by the child or by the parent, and so on. If you think about it, the individual profile for each child could build into a massive tome, and one of the most important things practitioners have to consider is how to create profiles that are detailed, meaningful and manageable. The question to ask is 'What do I keep?' You will remember that we discussed this in the chapter relating to significant moments.

In the previous chapter we also touched on conferencing when we talked about involving parents in the assessment of their own children. The term arose some years ago when teachers at the Centre for Language in Education (now known as the Centre for Literacy in Primary Education) (CLPE) started work on an important project about how to track and document children's development as speakers, readers and writers. The group of teachers became more and more aware of the role played by parents in their children's literacy development and devised a format where parents could have in-depth discussion with teachers about what their children did at home that influenced their development as speakers, readers and writers. This was known as the parent conference. They also developed a format where children could reflect on their own development as readers and writers, and this was known as the child conference. So the term 'conferencing' was born and added to the list of possible assessment tools used to gain a more complete picture of each learner.

Many nurseries and settings have some form of parent conference, often used as part of the settling-in process. At your own centre you may set aside a time when parents and carers of new pupils come in and talk with the headteacher, the class teacher or the key worker about the child's background and interests. Where this is well done the information gained is extremely useful in discovering children's existing knowledge and interests.

To illustrate this, here are some examples:

When a new child is registered for the nursery class the parent/carer is given a form and asked to complete it at the school. On the form, in addition to information like contact details, is a section asking questions about the child's life, interests and experience at home.

Here is the form completed for a Turkish child called Ozman. Ozman's mother speaks only Turkish so the school invited her to bring a translator with her. The key worker wrote down the things the translator said on behalf of Ozman's mother:

Please tell us something about any stories, rhymes, songs that your child knows and likes.	Ozman knows some nursery rhymes and he sings lots of pop songs. He knows Turkish songs. He doesn't like looking at books. He likes comics and he likes TV.
What things does your child like to do at home?	He loves cars and building things and watching telly. He likes to play with the boys next door. He loves his mum and dad and his brother and sister. He loves to go and stay with his nan. He loves to go on holiday to Turkey.
Please tell us about any things your child is scared of or doesn't like to do.	He tries to be tough and he says he is not scared of anything but he has a light on in his room at night – one of those night-lights. He hates to eat salad.
Is there anything special we should know about your child?	He is a lovely boy – very kind – very loving.

In another setting the whole process is done differently. All prospective parents are given a form to take home and fill in. The form only requires them to tick boxes.

Which of these things does your child like to do?	☐ Listen to stories ☐ Look at books ☐ Draw pictures ☐ Build things ☐ Make things out of junk materials ☐ Sing songs ☐ Watch television

85

	☐ Count
	☐ Play with water
	☐ Play with sand
	☐ Do messy things
	☐ Tidy up
	☐ Sort things out
Which of these things can your child already do?	☐ Dress him/herself
	☐ Put things away in the correct place
	☐ Write his or her name
	☐ Recognise his or her name
	☐ Recognise any other words
	☐ Count up to 5
	☐ Say how old s/he is
	☐ Follow simple instructions
What do you think your child is like? Can you write in the box all the things that make your child special? Think about things like how your child interacts with people, listens to you, etc. Tell us anything you like.	Selina is a very good child. She helps me at home and she is very loving. She makes friends easily and she is kind to them. She speaks only little English but she learns quickly. She will be a doctor one day.

You will have some views about the different approaches and might like to think about what sorts of message prospective parents get from each of these two approaches. Ozman's mother clearly has more opportunity to tell the school quite a lot about her child whereas Selina's mum only has one box in which she can write. All the other answers are pre-determined by the questions.

Collecting some 'baseline' information is common. In some schools and settings this is taken a step further and parents/carers, and sometimes even pupils, are invited to comment on what the child has learned over a period of time. Doing this adds another dimension to this summing up of achievement.

Involving children in profiling is a complex task and requires considerable thought and planning. Where it is done well children say interesting and revealing things and their comments or pieces of work add enormously to the sense of that child's achievement over a period of time.

Here are some examples of the comments made by children and written either by themselves or by the teacher or childcare worker acting as scribe:

IamgdatrIting

(5-year-old Alison wrote 'I am good at writing')

I like reading story books. I like making things. I like painting. I don't like writing. It is very hard.

(Written by 7-year-old Jasmin)

What do you like best at school?	I like playtime and I like it when we have stories.
What do you think you are good at?	I am good at drawing and I am good at making things and I am good at football.
What do you find hard?	Number work!

(Discussion with 6-year-old Melanie: transcribed by the teacher)

What do you like doing at nursery?	I like painting – and playing with the dolls – and making things – and my friends – and my teacher is lovely.
What have you learned at nursery?	I've learned to make things and to paint and to tidy up and to play nicely with my friends and to share and to take turns and not to fight and not to scribble.
What would you like to learn now?	I want to learn how to write my name and I want to learn how to colour in in the lines and I want to learn how to be a big girl.

(Discussion with 4-year-old Celebrity)

Involving parents in contributing their thoughts is something worth doing but it requires both sensitivity and tight organisation. Sensitivity is required because there may well be parents who find writing, or writing in English difficult and who might be embarrassed if this is known by the school or setting. Making translators available or offering to record things said by parents are possible ways round this. What is important is that the children of parents who may have little English or few writing skills are not disadvantaged in any way.

Organising for parents to contribute to profiles or records requires careful thought about how and when to invite parents in to do this. There are various alternatives which you as a group might explore. For example:

▷ Should you send the record form home?
▷ Should you invite parents in groups?
▷ Should you make individual appointments?
▷ How do you ensure that you consider the requirements of working parents, single parents, parents who prefer not to come out when it is dark, etc.?
▷ Should you provide a crèche?
▷ Should you provide translators and interpreters?

At one school the staff group decided to invite parents into the classes at the end of the school day. One teacher ran a crèche in the hall and one teacher went round helping parents complete the forms. There were translators present and some of the older children in the school were also available to help give out the forms.

In another school the parents or carers were met at the start of the school day and given a form and an adult explained what was wanted. Parents and carers were offered the help of local translators and parents took the forms away with them.

Here are some examples of the sorts of comments made by parents halfway through the reception year:

| What can you say about your child's interest in books and reading? | Hamish is still not very interested in reading although he does read the book he brings home. He knows lots of the stories off by heart and re-tells the story from the pictures, I think. He can recognise some words – his name, mum, dad and love! |

| Does your child show any interest in writing? | Hamish loves writing and writes endless lists. I can't read a word but he can so I suppose he is writing. |
| What changes have you seen in your child over this term? | He is much more confident and much happier. He loves coming to school and is exhausted – and hungry – when he gets home. He is much less angry and irritable than he was at the beginning of term. |

Hamish's teacher, reading these comments, realises that Hamish needs much more support in learning to be interested in books. Although he is making progress as a reader he is still not keen to read.

What does your child tell you about school and about what he does each day?	Teresa tells us about the things she has made. She tells us when the teacher says nice things about her work. She tells us that she does reading and writing and PE.
Please tell us about anything your child doesn't like about school.	She doesn't like dinners or dinnertime. She says there is lots of fighting and she is nervous of the playground. She doesn't like going to assemblies and she doesn't like writing.
Please tell us how your child has changed since she started in this class.	She comes home tired and irritable every day. All she wants to do is watch TV. She used to look at books and play when she was at home but now she doesn't want to do these things.

Teresa's teacher, reading these comments, is given much to think about. She knows, of course, that many children find school tiring, but she is bothered that this child is being turned off books and that lunchtimes and playtimes appear to be a trial for her.

You can see how inviting parents and children to contribute their voices adds enormously to the understanding educators can have of the progress and development of the children. You are reminded that learning, particularly in the early years, is holistic and that children are learning from everything that happens to them – in school and out.

The comments and observations made by children and parents come at the end of something – in the cases above at the end of a term. They can be regarded as forms of summative assessment and can be used to contribute to the records of children's progress being kept by teachers.

RECORD-KEEPING

Record-keeping is a fundamental part of all teaching and provides opportunities for many things – from tracking the progress of individual children to informing future teaching. Keeping records ensures that each class or setting has an accurate and up-to-date profile of individual children's learning which provides the basis for the reports to parents and carers. Records help teachers to monitor the progress of children and to intervene or seek expert help where necessary.

We started off this book with a statement about assessment being the process of gathering together evidence against which judgements can be made about each child's progress and development. We have been looking at all the different types of evidence that can be collected to contribute to the picture being developed of each child. Significant moments noted by adults, comments by the children, observations from their parents, observation notes, tick lists and notes made by all the adults concerned with the child all constitute evidence. Evidence is gathered carefully and economically. Many settings invite staff to jot down brief comments, dated, on sticky notes. You will develop your own systems, but do remember that whatever you do has to be manageable.

BUILDING A RECORD OF ACHIEVEMENT OR PROFILE

We offer you now a section of the record of achievement or profile of one child, showing progress across different areas of learning and over time.

We will look at the profile built up across all six learning areas for Ozman whom you met earlier in this chapter through what his mum said about him on entry to the nursery class. During his year in the reception class the teacher and teaching assistant, together with the language support teacher, built up a profile of him, using evidence from observations of significant moments, samples of his work, comments he made and comments made by the adults involved with him.

Personal, social and emotional development

September: Ozman is very noisy and boisterous in the classroom. He was seen shoving two smaller children and asked not to do it.

October: Spent a long time making a model out of found materials. Was very engrossed. Brought it to show me – very proud.

November: Did a wonderful intricate painting of an aeroplane and when asked how he managed to make it so realistic he said 'I looked hard with my eyes' (links to creative development).

December: Mum came to the school show. Ozman was one of the narrators. She told me that he loves coming to school and is 'getting better and better'.

Communications, language and literacy

September: Ozman is bilingual. Speaks English and Turkish. He is not yet reading and appears not very interested in books although he knows lots of songs, which he delights in singing very loudly.
(Reminder to ask mum if his hearing has been checked)
Language assistant added: He is bilingual and speaks English in class but Turkish to his friends in the playground. He is aware and proud of having 2 languages. He needs opportunities to demonstrate his skills as a linguist to the teachers and to the other children.

September: Wrote his name today using all 5 letters. 'Look – me! Ozman'

October: Made marks on paper – left to write, top to bottom, some letter-like shapes and several letters from his name. 'I'm writing my letter to my mum' he said.

October: Brought back the book he had taken home last night and his mum had written 'He told me the story by turning the pages and looking at the pictures'.

December: Can write his own name and that of some of his friends; mum, I, like, cars, etc.

Mathematical development

September: Counts fluently in English and Turkish, always with one to one correspondence. Very confident in handling numbers.

October: We were singing happy birthday to one of the children who had just turned 6 and he said 'When I am six both of us will make twelve'.

November: Becoming very interested in patterns. Makes patterns all the time and started commenting about number patterns. 'Look. When you count 5 and 5 and 5 the end goes 5 and 0 and 5.'

December: Mum says that he is very clever because he is 'always doing things with numbers'.

Knowledge and understanding of the world

September: Very interested in anything that moves – cars, buses, bicycles, boats, and aeroplanes. Draws pictures of them. Makes models. Chooses to play with small cars and ramps, boats in the water, etc.

October: After his mum had taken him to the Transport Museum he told the whole class what he had seen in minute detail.

November: Latest passion is things that turn. Perhaps a rotational schema? He draws lots of circles and is always making wheels. I talked to his mum about schemas and she is watching what he is doing at home. Mum reports that he is always turning round himself, makes his knife spin round on the table, loves to go on the roundabout in the park and draws loads of circles at home.

December: The language support teacher read him a story about a spinning top and said it was the first book she had found that had him totally engrossed. He took it home. He needs access to more books with themes that interest him.

Creative development

September: Spent a very long time building with a friend using Lego. At the end told the class he had made a castle.

October: Still interested in building and built a massive structure in the playground using milk crates and planks. Said it was a 'magic potter castle'. (Influence of Harry Potter?)

November: His passion for rotation is emerging in his drawings and paintings where there are many spirals and circles.

Physical development

September: Ozman is a very active child who finds being in the classroom very difficult. He really needs space to move around. Mum says he is impossible indoors. Always wants to be in the park or running around somewhere.

October: He is getting more able to use his considerable physical skills and refine his fine motor skills. He is cutting and using pencils and paintbrushes with much greater facility than a month ago.

November: His fine motor skills are impressive. He uses a range of tools at the woodwork bench; often paints using thick and thin brushes, makes very neat letter and number shapes.

December: He has discovered dancing and seems to bring together his passion for rotation and his sense of pattern when he moves to music in the hall.

These are brief extracts from a profile being built up o/ You can see how the selection of significant moments ⟨ comments from Ozman himself and from his mother c⟨ reader getting a real sense of this child's learning an/ You will realise that all of this involves formative as⟨ everyday judgements about children's learning and d⟨ observing them, listening to them, and talking t⟨

adults involved with them. By sifting through the mass of evidence that it is possible to gather together, looking for indications of significant developments, a profile can be built up and this will not only provide a wonderful record for individual children and their families and carers, but will also help the teacher with summative assessment. This is done when the teacher uses all the carefully selected and sifted information to construct a summative record in the form of a report to parents.

SUMMING UP

✔ All those involved in the education of children need to devise systems of record-keeping. Records need to be kept up to date and they need to be manageable. It is tempting to believe that you can keep a lot of information in your head and don't need to make notes. You may, in fact, have a wonderful memory but with so many children to monitor you will, inevitably, lose some detail unless you record things. What is more, you may not always be available and it is important that records are accessible to other workers when you are not present. It will inevitably take time to develop a system of knowing what to record, where to record it and how to store it. This is why understanding about significant moments is so important as a potential tool for managing record-keeping.

✔ The records you keep should show how each child is progressing and highlight both achievements and areas for improvement. If you go back to the record of achievement above you will find some examples of both.

✔ Records may contain information gathered from children themselves, their parents and all those working with the child. They can include information gathered from observations, discussions, directed tasks and tests, where these are required by your setting.

✔ Records should be ongoing and cumulative and linked to evidence. This means that saying things like 'John is getting better at writing' means far less than a more evidence-based statement such as 'In his writing John demonstrated that he is able to . . .', particularly where the evidence (the actual piece of writing) is present with the statement.

✔ The records should be made available to the receiving teacher. Obvious as this sounds, there is a real danger that records are not passed on and that children are required to repeat what they have already done. The starting point for each educator should be the current knowledge and understanding of each pupil.

GLOSSARY

Baseline information	In this context it refers to information gathered about the child on entry to the school or setting.
Cumulative	When talking of records this means that they should follow on from one another to build a complete picture of the child.
Evidence	In assessment terms evidence is anything that shows the progress of the child. It may include what the child said or did or made, for example.
Learning areas	These are defined in the Foundation Stage Curriculum and refer to aspects of learning grouped into clusters.
Record of achievement	This is a record of the child's development and progress made up of different types of evidence.
Sticky notes	Squares of coloured paper with sticky patches on the back at the top.

Chapter 8

Reporting and accountability

- ✔ In this chapter we look at what the statutory assessment and reporting requirements are for teachers in England.

- ✔ We look too at how you should prepare and present reports for parents.

- ✔ We look at some sample reports and, to end the chapter, we have a laugh.

One of the most familiar things about assessment is the school report. Children have been bringing them home for generations. But what is the purpose of this report? Why do teachers and other educators write reports? The answer is that all of us involved in the lives of children are accountable both to headteachers, line managers, OFSTED inspectors and others in positions of authority, and also to the parents and carers of the pupils themselves. Ideally we are also accountable to the pupils. One of the ways of discharging this accountability is to send home reports on pupils' progress.

In your day-to-day life you meet parents or carers when they bring children to and collect them from your setting. There is, in all probability, some exchange of informal and ongoing information about how the child is getting on. In the nurseries of Reggio Emilia this system of day-to-day contact is formalised, particularly for the parents of babies and toddlers. The staff in each nursery recognise that parents who are working or studying are often missing out on those vital key moments in a child's life – for example, when the child takes her first step or says her first word. They also realise that parents don't know what the child has done during the day and thus may offer the child inappropriate things to do at home. Examples of this are where the child has slept all afternoon and clearly should not be put to bed on arriving back home or where a child has refused all food and needs to eat before doing anything else.

The way in which staff deal with this is very organised, informative and sometimes moving. Each child has a plastic wallet displayed on the wall of the room where he or she is based. Staff update these daily with brief comments like 'Took his first step today. Bravo, Giulio!' or 'Ate pasta with peas and some fruit for lunch' or 'Drew pictures, did some cutting and sticking, played with Antonia'. These snippets of information are wonderful in that they help parents feel part of the child's life and progress and in that they help bridge the links between home and school or setting.

In England teachers have a statutory obligation to report to the child's parents annually, in writing, commenting on the child's performance and achievements during the year. Reports must be built up of short statements and must refer both to achievements and to weaknesses. Teachers must report not only on children's academic progress but also on their behaviour and their attitudes. Each report must also mention attendance over the year.

Parents of children in the Foundation Stage (aged 3 to nearly 6, in the nursery or reception classes) are to receive reports discussing progress in each of the six learning areas. Children in Key Stage 1 (from 6 to 7 or in Years 1 and 2) are to get reports relating to National Curriculum subjects.

EXAMPLES OF REPORTS

There is a definite skill to report writing and it is something that not everyone finds easy. There have also been recent changes in the thinking around reports and these are very much in the interests of parents and children. Take the example of a report written about a child some twenty years ago and compare it with the one that follows:

Child's name:	Sammy	**Age:** 5
Reading	Good	
Writing	Good but needs to pay attention to letter formation	
Number work	Good but her work is messy	

History	She must learn not to talk in class
Geography	She must learn not to talk in class
Punctuality	Could do better

Now read the report for Ozman's parents, prepared by the teacher but drawing on notes and comments from the teaching assistant, the language support assistant, Ozman himself and his mum. You will remember Ozman from the previous chapter.

Pupil's name: Ozman **School Year:** 2003–4 (Reception Class)

Personal, social and emotional development
Ozman started the school year as a boisterous, noisy and sometimes aggressive child. His mother told us in his entry profile that he was not nearly as confident as he appeared and we became aware, as he settled into the routines of the class, that he had considerable intellectual skills and was able to channel his limitless energy into many activities. By the end of the year he was one of the more mature children in the class, often willing to help other children and always an involved member of any group. His progress in this area has really been remarkable and he is now helpful, reliable and an asset to the class.

Communications, language and literacy
On entry to the class Ozman was already bilingual in English and Turkish and the language support assistant pointed out his confidence in this area. He showed great pride in his language and culture and often talked to the class about how things in Turkish are similar to or different from English. He is a talkative and gregarious little boy who always has something to say. He entertained the whole class with his descriptions of what he had seen on his visit to the Transport Museum.

He started the year as a reluctant reader and learning to read has been more of a struggle than a pleasure for him. When he managed to re-tell a story from a known book for the first time his confidence grew and he is now able to read some of the class books, using a range of cues to help him work out new or unfamiliar words. As his confidence and his exposure to more books and stories increases, his reading will develop.

He enjoys making marks on paper although his writing is not yet readable by others. He uses some recognisable letters in his writing together with some letter-like symbols. He sometimes puts spaces between his words – but not consistently – and the stories he tells or dictates are far more interesting than the ones he manages to write. He clearly finds the physical skills of writing slow him down. In Year 1 he will need much encouragement to help him develop into an independent writer.

Mathematical development

Ozman is very confident and able in this area. He is able to count way beyond 20 in both English and Turkish and also able to solve number problems, sometimes in his head. His interest in patterns has helped him pay attention to how number systems work. He works on the top table for mathematics and really enjoys this area. He has had experience of doing some work around measurement and capacity, shape and space, counting and money. He sometimes has problems writing the numerals correctly and often has to be told to slow down.

Creative development

Ozman is an inventive, creative and enthusiastic child. He loves movement, music and dance and would happily spend all day listening to music and moving to it. He also enjoys all aspects of painting and drawing and has produced some beautiful pictures, most of which he has taken home to put on the walls of his flat. He is very interested in three-dimensional work and often builds things on a small scale in the classroom and on a larger scale in the playground. The thing he enjoyed most this year was building a massive 'robot' out of large packing boxes and decorating it. This was displayed in the entrance hall with his name and age against it. He was very proud of this work – and deservedly so.

Knowledge and understanding of the world

Ozman is a little boy with many interests. During this year he has explored things that spin, magnets, patterns, transport and building. He tends to have passions that last for several months during which time he explores something in lots of different ways. He shows little interest in animals or in art. He really did not enjoy the visit we made to the Tate Modern – other than the journey there!

Physical development

Ozman is a tall and strong boy who finds the requirements of being in a small classroom very difficult. Some days he cannot wait to get out into the playground. His ability to sit quietly has improved but he is one of many children who really need room to run around. He is very skilled both in terms of gross movements and fine. He can run, kick a ball, catch and throw. He cannot skip and disdains it as 'for girls'! His fine motor skills are excellent and he is able to use a range of tools to cut and write and draw and paint and stick. He has made models out of junk materials and out of woodwork. He has enjoyed cooking and planting seeds.

Attendance: 300 out of a possible 312 attendances
Unauthorised absences: 0

General comments
This has been a good year for Ozman. He has developed his confidence and his skills and become a liked and valued member of the class.

THE LANGUAGE OF REPORTS

If you read through this report carefully you will notice that care has been taken in writing the comments to make sure that they are both meaningful and accessible. By this we mean that the things written should tell the receiving parents something about the child's development and something about what the child might still need to do or learn. Parents don't need to receive meaningless comments like 'good' or 'could do better'. The comments must be specific about just what it is that the child has achieved and what it is that the child still needs to do. The term 'accessible' suggests that the report should be written in language which is reasonably jargon-free so that most parents – who are unlikely to be educationalists – can understand what is being said. Some jargon comments might illustrate this:

- ▶ Peter is struggling with using graphophonic cues.
- ▶ Jasmin is able to hypothesise, synthesise and analyse.
- ▶ Bab enjoys exploring genre.

DEALING WITH DIFFICULT REPORTS

Writing a report about a child who has made reasonable progress over a period of time is relatively simple compared to writing a report about a child who has been the object of worry and concern throughout the year. Many people find it extremely difficult to tell parents negative things about their children. You might like to consider what you would put in a report for the children described below.

Maria has been in the nursery all year. She came with very little English and leaves with very little English. She was isolated in the class throughout the year and did not manage to make any friendships because her only ways of interacting seemed to be very aggressive. She pushed and shoved; took things she wanted; occasionally bit and kicked the other children and used a wide range of extremely abusive language (almost her total English vocabulary!) when reprimanded or stopped. She showed little or no interest in books, reading, writing or counting. She moved from one activity to another, seemingly unable to spend any time getting involved in anything with any degree of concentration. She does enjoy singing and music and this is the only session during which she cooperates. Her parents are tired, overworked, and unable to control her or her four older brothers and struggling to learn any English. How do you communicate with them?

There is no simple answer to this. The team working with Maria spent several hours discussing what they might put on her report so that her parents would take her problems seriously and also understand more about her needs. They wanted her to receive some appropriate help and support in the reception class and needed to find positive things to focus on so that at least some of the report would be optimistic. They decided to abandon the standard format and settled for this:

Name of child: Maria   **Class:** nursery

Maria came into the nursery at the beginning of the year and it took her a long time to settle. She found it difficult to interact with the other children and needed considerable support over the year to learn not to hurt the other children.

She is a bilingual child speaking Greek and English but her spoken English needs to improve if she is to do well at school. She would benefit from hearing songs and stories in English and from watching children's programmes on television. When she goes into the reception class she will benefit from having the support of a specialist language assistant who works with the children two mornings a week.

She really enjoys music and singing and is beginning to know lots of songs by heart. Songs may provide a good way into helping her with her English and also a good way into helping her learn to read. In the reception class they will help her by making some books particularly for her, which contain the words of the songs she knows. She loves the two books made for her in the nursery and is bringing these home to show you. Please encourage her to 'sing' the songs to you.

If Maria can come to school more regularly and arrive on time she will benefit from the routine and from being with the other children all the time. We would be happy to talk to you about what will help her.

101

SAMPLE REPORTS

We include here an article from the *Times Educational Supplement* telling readers what should go into a good primary school report. (The advice is for pupils at Key Stage 1, but you might find it interesting reading.)

The contents of a good report for primary schools

A comprehensive report will inform parents truthfully of their child's achievements and offer advice on giving useful help at home. Follow these guidelines and statutory requirements will be easily covered.

Subject	Contents of narrative
Language/Literacy/ English	Brief outline of learning experiences
Reading, writing, spelling and handwriting	What the pupil has achieved (NC working level and/or where the pupil is with relation to the cohort/age)
Speaking and listening	Future development and targets, and how parents can help
Numeracy	Brief outline of learning experiences What the pupil has achieved (NC working level and/or where the pupil is with relation to the cohort/age) Future development and targets, and how parents can help
Science	Brief outline of learning experiences What the pupil has achieved (NC working level and/or where the pupil is with relation to the cohort/age) Future development and targets, and how parents can help
All other subjects	Brief outline of learning experiences What the pupil has achieved Future development and targets
Personal and social education	Include a combination of any of the following: Progress, Behaviour, Effort. Concentration, Cooperative skills, Interest, Attitude, Confidence, Personal targets, Attendance, Organisation/planning, Punctuality Homework

And here is an example of what is offered as a model Key Stage 1 report by the QCA.

Name: Nabeel Haq   Year: 2

PROGRESS REVIEW

2002/2003

The purpose of this review is to:

- provide you with details of the programmes of study for key stage 1.
- provide you with a full update on your child's progress in the core subjects of English, mathematics and science and a brief summary of progress in the foundation subjects.
- share the next stage of your child's learning by looking at areas for development.
- note under the heading 'Personal and Social Development', relevant information such as your child's behaviour and attitudes to peers and adults.

ATTENDANCE

Number of sessions in the year (1 session = ½ day)	308
Number of authorised absences e.g. illness, health appointments, holidays	5
Number of unauthorised absences (Reason unknown)	0
Number of late arrivals	3

Class Teacher: Mrs A J Smith

103

End of key stage 1 assessment results 2003

Name: Nabeel Haq

ENGLISH

Teacher assessment results

Speaking and listening	level 3
Reading	level 4+
Writing	level 3

Task and test results

Reading task	level 2A
Reading test	level 3
Writing task	level 2A

MATHEMATICS

Teacher assessment result

	level 2C

Task or test result

Mathematics task/test	level 2C

SCIENCE

Teacher assessment result

	level 2B

There are no tests or tasks in science for key stage 1

Level 1 and W (meaning working towards
level 1) represent achievement below the nationally expected
standard for most 7-year-olds. Level 2 is divided into three grades
– 2A, 2B and 2C. Level 2B represents achievement at the
nationally expected standard for most 7-year-olds. Levels
3 and 4+ represent achievement above the nationally
expected standard for most 7-year-olds.

Programmes of study

During key stage 1 your child has followed the national curriculum in the core and foundation subjects. The following table gives you an indication of what the programme of study requires for each subject.

English

Children learn to speak confidently and listen to what others have to say. They begin to read and write independently and with enthusiasm. They use language to explore their own experiences and imaginary worlds.

Mathematics

Children develop their knowledge and understanding of mathematics through practical activity, exploration and discussion. They learn to count, read, write and order numbers to 100 and beyond. They develop a range of mental calculation skills and use these confidently in different settings. They learn about shape and space through practical activity which builds on their immediate environment. They begin to grasp mathematical language, using it to talk about their methods and explain their reasoning when solving problems.

Science

Children observe, explore and ask questions about living things, materials and phenomena. They begin to work together to collect evidence to help them answer questions and to link this to simple scientific ideas. They evaluate evidence and consider whether tests or comparisons are fair. They use reference materials to find out more about scientific ideas. They share their ideas and communicate them using scientific language, drawings, charts and tables.

Design and technology

Children learn how to think imaginatively and talk about what they like and dislike when designing and making. They build on their early childhood experiences of investigating objects around them. They explore how familiar things work and talk about, draw and model their ideas for new products. They learn how to design and make safely and could start to use ICT as part of their designing and making. They learn to identify what they could have done differently or how they could improve their work in the future.

ICT

Children explore ICT and learn to use it confidently and with purpose to achieve specific outcomes. They start to use ICT to develop their ideas and record their creative work. They become familiar with hardware and software.

History

Children learn about people's lives and lifestyles. They find out about significant men, women, children and events from the recent and more distant past, including those from both Britain and the wider world. They listen and respond to stories and use sources of information to help them ask and answer questions. They learn how the past is different from the present.

Geography

Children investigate their local area and a contrasting area in the United Kingdom or abroad, finding out about the environment in both areas and the people who live there. They also begin to learn about the wider world. They carry out geographical enquiry inside and outside the classroom. In doing this they ask geographical questions about people, places and environments, and use geographical skills and resources such as maps and photographs.

Art and design

Children develop their creativity and imagination by exploring the visual, tactile and sensory qualities of materials and processes. They learn about the role of art, craft and design in their environment. They begin to understand colour, shape and space and pattern and texture and use them to represent their ideas and feelings.

Music

Children listen carefully and respond physically to a wide range of music. They play musical instruments and sing a variety of songs from memory, adding accompaniments and creating short compositions, with increasing confidence, imagination and control. They explore and enjoy how sounds and silence can create different moods and effects.

PE

Children build on their natural enthusiasm for movement, using it to explore and learn about their world. They start to work and play with other children in pairs and small groups. By watching, listening and experimenting, they develop their skills in movement and coordination, and enjoy expressing and testing themselves in a variety of situations.

RE

[To be determined by the locally agreed syllabus; the following is an example only.] Children learn about Christian and Jewish festivals and the people and stories associated with them. They explore their meanings and importance for people today. They begin to understand the significance and use of symbols in religion, and discuss their own ideas on this.

PSHE and citizenship

Children learn about themselves as developing individuals and as members of their communities, building on their own experiences and on the early learning goals for personal, social and emotional development. They learn the basic rules and skills for keeping themselves healthy and safe and for behaving well. They have opportunities to show they can take responsibility for themselves and their environment. They begin to learn about their own and other people's feelings and become aware of views, needs and rights of other children and older people. As members of a class and school community, they learn social skills such as how to share, take turns, play, help others, resolve simple arguments and resist bullying. They begin to take an active part in the life of their school and its neighbourhood.

ENGLISH

Progress this year

Nabeel can now speak clearly, fluently and confidently to different people on a range of topics. He is still a little shy when talking to other children he doesn't know, but this is improving. His listening skills have also improved and he is now able to answer fairly complex questions on what he has just heard. In drama, he enjoys sharing his ideas, but is often quiet when performing.

107

Nabeel enjoys reading and is now able to read aloud fluently and with expression. He particularly enjoys reading books about ghosts. His handwriting is improving, and he usually uses joined up writing. He has lots of ideas for his story writing but often rushes which means his sentences are often incomplete.

Nabeel should be pleased with his progress in English this year. He has established a good foundation for key stage 2.

Targets

Nabeel should concentrate when writing to make sure he gets all of his ideas onto paper in a clear way. He also needs to practise speaking in front of people so that he can perform his ideas more confidently in drama.

MATHEMATICS

Progress

Nabeel has tried very hard in mathematics in the last year to overcome the difficulties he has had in the past. He is now able to work with numbers up to 100, though he can still get confused beyond 100. He is able to perform addition with two digit numbers on paper, and has improved his mental addition skills. However, he still struggles with subtraction and is still only able to calculate subtractions using counters as an aid. He has learnt his 2, 3 and 5 times tables, though it is not yet clear that he fully understands what he has learnt.

Nabeel is able to read information from tables and charts and his work on the class survey showed that he is very good at constructing his own charts from the data he collected.

Nabeel is much stronger spatially than numerically, and his spatial awareness skills are very advanced for his age. He can name and describe all the common 2D and 3D shapes and is able to visualise rotation and reflection without aids.

Targets

Nabeel needs to continue to work hard on his number skills so that he can solve numerical problems. In particular he needs to ensure he understands the number work he is asked to do, and asks when he does not, rather than just trying to memorise facts.

SCIENCE

Progress

This term Nabeel has learnt how to collect evidence by making observations and taking measurements. He has also been able to describe if a test has been made fairly and why. He has improved his knowledge of scientific vocabulary and uses words appropriately to describe events and observations.

Nabeel enjoyed looking at the differences between living and non-living things. He particularly enjoyed the class activity of growing cress.

Targets

Nabeel needs to think carefully before experiments about what he thinks is going to happen before rushing to complete the experiment.

ACHIEVEMENTS AND AREAS FOR IMPROVEMENT IN FOUNDATION SUBJECTS

INFORMATION & COMMUNICATION TECHNOLOGY

Achievements

- Nabeel can use the computer to retrieve information, for example from a CD-Rom.
- He can write instructions to control the floor turtle.

Areas for improvement

- Nabeel needs to practise using the computer to present information.

DESIGN & TECHNOLOGY

Achievements

- Nabeel often generates exciting design ideas based on his experience at home.
- He uses pictures and words in a lively way when he is clarifying those ideas.
- He can use a variety of tools with some accuracy, explaining why he has chosen those particular tools.

109

- He can talk about what he found difficult about a project and suggest ways of improving the final product.

Areas for improvement

- Nabeel finds it difficult to share and develop ideas with others.
- He finds 3D modelling difficult and could spend some of the time he devotes to pictures and words on 3D work instead.

HISTORY

Achievements

- Nabeel was able to recognise the similarities and differences between different periods of time when we studied ancient Egypt.
- He is often able to explain the reasons why events in the past happened, for example what factors led to the gunpowder plot.

Areas for improvement

- Nabeel has difficulty with putting dates in chronological order and needs to focus on this.

GEOGRAPHY

Achievements

- Nabeel is able to describe and compare the physical and human features of two different places. He showed this most notably in his report comparing Alresford and a village in St Lucia.
- He is very good at using and drawing maps.

Areas for improvement

- Nabeel needs to learn and use geographical vocabulary when describing places.

RELIGIOUS EDUCATION

Achievements

- Nabeel has studied Christianity and Judaism and can explain features of their festivals and celebrations such as how light is used as a symbol.
- He can listen to and comment on others' views.

Areas for improvement

- Nabeel should try to put forward his own ideas to others in a more confident way.

PHYSICAL EDUCATION

Achievements

- Nabeel shows control, coordination and a sound understanding of what to achieve when using tactics in games and performing gymnastic activity sequences and short dances he has designed.
- He works energetically, often on his own, and is keen to make progress describing what he does well and identifying what he can do to improve.

Areas for improvement

- Nabeel's work will improve when he can work better in a team or group.

ART & DESIGN

Achievements

- Nabeel has worked successfully with a variety of materials and processes. His work with modelling clay was particularly pleasing.
- He is able to discuss differences and similarities between his work and that of others in the class.

Areas for improvement

- Nabeel needs to think more about how he can develop his ideas further.

MUSIC

Achievements

- Nabeel is developing his singing voice and is becoming more accurate at repeating tunes he has heard.
- He has successfully created musical patterns on the keyboard to use in compositions.

Areas for improvement

- Nabeel needs to learn how to evaluate and make improvements to his work.

PSHE & CITIZENSHIP

Achievements

- Nabeel has produced some very good display work on health and safety issues.
- During work on 'Respect for property', he showed that he understands why we must take responsibility for our own belongings and those of other people. He has a strong sense of right and wrong and understands the consequences of disrespectful behaviours such as theft and vandalism.
- He is able to share and take turns in activities when working as a member of a group.

Areas for improvement

- Nabeel can find it difficult to contribute to group discussions and should practise speaking in front of other people to develop confidence.

CHILD'S COMMENTS

I have enjoyed most of my classes, especially art as I like drawing and painting. I like reading books and like English as I like talking about books I have read. I liked growing plants in science and had a lot of fun looking after my plant and watching it get big.

TEACHER'S COMMENTS

Nabeel has made great progress this year and has improved his skills in many areas. He enjoys school, despite sometimes finding it difficult to work with other children. He is a likeable child, though he still needs to develop his confidence. I wish him every success for key stage 2.

(www.qcq.org.uk/downloads/ks1_sample_report2.rtf)

You will realise that there is much to admire in this detailed report. The parent reading it will have a very clear idea of just what has been done in the child's class during the year and will have a picture of how well the child has done. Achievements are indicated but so are things to improve and, following the current trend in education, targets are set.

You may question how realistic it would be for all teachers to complete records as detailed as this for thirty or more children.

COULD DO BETTER!

The chances are that on your old school reports you will find some comments which do not reveal the person you believe yourself to be. The following comments are drawn from a book called *Could Do Better: School Reports of the Great and Good*, edited by C. Hurley and published in 2004. Have a laugh!

Jon Snow's Latin report

'One feels that he would never have been in the lowest of the fifths, had he learnt to be humble and not to question every point'

Sue Lawley's PE report

'I do believe Susan has glue in her plimsolls'

Beryl Bainbridge's English report

'Though her written work is the product of an obviously lively imagination, it is a pity that her spelling derives from the same source'

Harry Enfield's Science report

'Perhaps his science will become more scientific next term'

Alan Coren's Physics report

'Coren's grasp of elementary dynamics is truly astonishing. Had he lived in an earlier aeon, I have little doubt but that the wheel would now be square and the principle of the lever just one more of man's impossible dreams'

Jilly Cooper's General report

'Jilly has set herself an extremely low standard which she has failed to maintain'

Alan Rusbridger

'He has been very argumentative and contradictory this term. A certain degree of intellectual independence is quite healthy for a boy of his age, but when it comes to dismissing large numbers of facts as irrelevant and bringing in every type of specious argument to try and disprove them, I feel he has overstepped the mark'

Peter Cook

'An unruffled temperament who has had considerable influence, especially in his own cultural field. He has qualities, not least a certain elusiveness – which should render him a most useful member of the Foreign Service'

Jeremy Paxman's Housemaster's report

'His stubbornness is in his nature, and could be an asset when directed to sound ends. But his flying off the handle will only mar his efforts, and he must learn tact while not losing his outspokenness'

Stephen Fry's Headmaster's report

'He has glaring faults and they have certainly glared at us this term'

Richard Briers

'It would seem that Briers thinks he is running the school and not me. If this attitude persists one of us will have to leave'

These extracts have obviously been written by skilled and witty teachers! Perhaps we should all aim for perceptive, witty, insightful comments like some of these.

SUMMING UP

In this chapter we have looked at what we need to do in order to fulfil statutory requirements to report to parents and to be accountable to governors and others. We have examined a range of styles of reporting and looked at a very detailed and informative report but questioned the possibility of being able to do such a report for each of thirty children in a class.

Chapter 9

Conclusion

Hopefully you have read through the previous eight chapters and found in them things that interested you and offered you information that will be both relevant and useful. Although many people shudder when they hear the word 'assessment', it is, in fact, one of the most important things we do when we work with children, and if used sensibly it is both revealing and fascinating.

It is important to remember that whatever the age of the children you are observing, each child comes to you with a unique history rich in experience. You have no access to that experience unless you are prepared to spend time getting to know the child. Sometimes this is extremely difficult. You may have twenty-nine other children wanting your attention; the child may speak a language you don't know; the child may be very withdrawn and silent or very angry and aggressive. But finding out as much as possible about each child is the only way in which you can successfully plan a programme for that child (and all the others in the class) to promote learning.

Liz Brooker, in her book *Starting School – Young Children Learning Cultures* (2002), describes how a reception class teacher tried to find out about the children in her class and focused on how they communicated, how independent they were, how they related to one another and how they tackled situations. On first reading, this all sounds fine, but an in-depth analysis of what the teacher learned from this showed distinct biases related to the dominant culture. It is important for all of us to remember that there are variations between groups and within groups in styles of communication (Should I make eye contact? Do I speak to this person?), expectations of children, ways of relating and so on. So how should we set about finding out as much as we can about the children when they come to us?

Dodie works in a reception class in an inner city school where fifty different languages are spoken. Most of the children coming into her class have spent time in the nursery class at the same school. She told us what she does.

I read all the records I get from the nursery class because they have been written for me and they give me a clear idea of what each child has had experience of in school. Each record contains a written statement from both the parent and the child and each parent completes a form on the child's entry to school. This tells me something about likes and dislikes, fears and passions. I work closely with the teaching assistant and with the special support teacher and we each take a group of children in the first weeks of term. These are our key children and we observe them closely and at the end of each day meet together to share our observations. We are looking primarily to see if the children appear to have settled into the new environment. We look to see if any of them are silent, withdrawn, aggressive, fearful or passive. We note who they play with and talk to, what they choose to do and enjoy doing. We note any leaps in learning – perhaps the first time the child volunteers an answer to questions.

In the following weeks we start paying attention to the work they produce and the objects or artefacts they make. We look to see if their attempts at writing include letters or letter-like shapes from the languages they encounter at home. (We have a list of each child and the languages spoken or read at home.) It is easier for us because the nursery staff have done all the hard work, really! When a new child joins the class we ensure we have time to talk to the parents and ensure that we have another speaker of the language with us where this is applicable. We try and make the parent know that we are only interested in supporting the child's learning and development and that we are not judging anyone's background or experience. So far it seems to be working.

Dodie is clear about the value of paying attention to what has gone before, recognising its importance in the life of each child and using it as the basis for planning.

In her chapter 'Observing Children' (1998) Mary Jane Drummond writes:

We have seen how observing children, if we do it carefully, attentively, thoughtfully, generously, can give us insights into the richness of their learning. There are other important reasons for observing, trying to make sense of what we see: these are to do with the responsibilities of the adults who care for and educate young children. Young children's awesome capacity for learning imposes a massive responsibility on early years educators to support, enrich and extend that learning. Everything we know about children's learning imposes on us an obligation to do whatever we can to foster and develop it: the extent to which we succeed in providing environments in which young children's learning can flourish. We cannot know if the environment we set up and the activities we provide for young children are doing what they should, unless we watch carefully, to keep track of the learning as and when it takes place.

(1998: 105)

These words provide a fitting conclusion to this book. We need to remember that we do children a disservice if we fail to observe them closely and use what we learn from this to help them move ahead in their learning and development.

Bibliography

Athey, C. (1990) *Extending Thought in Young Children.* London: Paul Chapman Publishing.

Axline, V. (1964) *Dibs: In Search of Self.* Harmondsworth: Penguin Books.

Baker, R. (1983) 'Refugees: An Overview of an International Problem', in Baker, R. (ed.) *The Psychosocial Problems of Refugees.* London: The British Refugee Council.

Brooker, L. (2002) *Starting School – Young Children Learning Cultures.* Buckingham and Philadelphia: Open University Press.

Bruner, J. (1966) *Towards a Theory of Instruction.* Cambridge, MA: Belknap Press of Harvard University Press.

Butt, J. and Box, L. (1998) *Family Centred – a Study of the Use of Family Centres by Black Families.* London: Racial Equality Unit.

Clarke, S. (2001) *Unlocking Formative Assessment: Practical Strategies for Enhancing Pupils' Learning in the Primary Classroom.* London: Hodder and Stoughton.

Crace, John (2003) 'Heaven and Helsinki', *The Guardian*, 16 September.

Department of Education and Science (1990) *Starting with Quality: The Rumbold Report of the Committee of Enquiry into the Quality of Educational Experiences Offered to Three and Four Year Olds.* London: HMSO.

Donaldson, M. (1978) *Children's Minds.* London: Fontana Press.

Draper, L. and Duffy, B. (2001) 'Working with Parents', in Pugh, G. *Contemporary Issues in the Early Years: Working Collaboratively for Children*, 3rd edition. London: Paul Chapman Publishing.

Drummond, M. J. (1998) 'Observing Children' in Smidt, S. (ed.) *The Early Years: A Reader.* London and New York: Routledge.

Fisher, J. (1999) *Starting from the Child? Teaching and Learning from 4 to 8.* Buckingham and Philadelphia: Open University Press.

Geertz, C. (1973) *The Interpretation of Cultures*. New York: Basic Books, Inc.

Greco, P. (1962) cited in Williams, C. and Kamii, C., 'How Do Children Learn by Handling Objects?', *Young Children*, November 1986, pp. 23–6.

Hall, N. (1999) 'Young Children, Play and Literacy: Engagement in Realistic Uses of Literacy', in Marsh, J. and Hallet, E. (eds) *Desirable Literacies*. London: Paul Chapman Publishing.

Hancock, R. and Cox, A. (2003) 'I Can Sing a Rainbow: Parents and Children under Three at Tate Britain, London', in Devereux, J. and Miller, L. (eds) *Working with Children in the Early Years*. London: David Fulton/Open University.

Holland, P. (2003) *We Don't Play with Guns Here: War, Weapon and Superhero Play in the Early Years*. Maidenhead and Philadelphia: Open University Press.

Hurley, C. (ed.) (2004) *Could Do Better: School Reports of the Great and Good*. Simon & Schuster.

Hurst, V. (1991) *Planning for Early Learning*. London: Paul Chapman Publishing.

Hutchin, V. (1999) *Right from the Start: Effective Planning and Assessment in the Early Years*. London: Hodder and Stoughton.

Hutchin, V. (2000) *Tracking Significant Achievement in the Early Years*, 2nd edition. London: Hodder and Stoughton.

Hyder, T. (1998) 'Supporting Refugee Children in the Early Years', in Rutter, J. and Jones, C. (eds) (1998) *Refugee Education: Mapping the Field*. Stoke-on-Trent: Trentham Books.

Isaacs, S. (1960) *Intellectual Growth in Young Children*. London: Routledge and Kegan Paul.

Lansdown, B. and Lancaster, Y.P. (2001) 'Promoting Children's Welfare by Respecting Their Rights', in Pugh, G. (2001) *Contemporary Issues in the Early Years: Working Collaboratively for Children*, 3rd edition. London: Paul Chapman Publishing.

Lansdown, G. (1996) 'The United Nations Convention on the Rights of the Child – Progress in the United Kingdom', in Nutbrown, C. (ed.) (1996) *Children's Rights and Early Education*. London: Paul Chapman Publishing.

McClellan, D. and Katz, L. (1992) 'Young Children's Social Development: A Checklist Adapted from Assessing the Social Development of Young Children: A Checklist of Social Attributes', in *Dimensions of Early Childhood* pp. 9–10.

Nash, M. (1967) 'Machine Age Maya', in Rogoff, B. (1990) *Apprenticeship in Thinking: Cognitive Development in Social Context*. New York and Oxford: Oxford University Press.

Nutbrown, C. (1994) *Threads of Thinking: Young Children Learning and the Role of Early Education*. London: Paul Chapman Publishing.

Nutbrown, C. (ed.) (1996) *Children's Rights and Early Education*. London: Paul Chapman Publishing.

Nutbrown, C. (2001) 'Watching and Learning: The Tools of Assessment', in Pugh, G. (2001) *Contemporary Issues in the Early Years: Working Collaboratively for Children*, 3rd edition. London: Paul Chapman Publishing.

O'Hara, M. (2000) *Teaching 3–8: Meeting the Standards for Initial Teacher Training and Induction*. London and New York: Continuum.

Organisation for Economic Cooperation and Development (OECD) (2003) Unesco Report on Educational Attainment.

Pahl, K. (1999) *Transformations: Meaning Making in Nursery Education*. Stoke-on-Trent: Trentham Books.

Piaget, J. and Inhelder, B. (1969) *The Psychology of the Child*. London: Routledge and Kegan Paul.

Pugh, G. (2001) *Contemporary Issues in the Early Years: Working Collaboratively for Children*, 3rd edition. London: Paul Chapman Publishing.

Qualifications and Curriculum Authority (QCA) (2000) *Curriculum Guidance for the Foundation Stage*. London: QCA.

Rogoff, B. (1990) *Apprenticeship in Thinking: Cognitive Development in Social Context*. New York and Oxford: Oxford University Press.

Rogoff, B. and Lave, J. (1999) *Everyday Cognition: Development in Social Context*. Cambridge, MA and London: Harvard University Press.

Schweinhart, L. *et al.* (1993) *Significant Benefits*. Ypsilanti, MI: High Scope Press.

Smidt, S. (ed.) (1998) *The Early Years: A Reader*. London and New York: Routledge.

Steele, M. *et al.* (2000) *Strengthening Families: Strengthening Communities: An Inclusive Parent Programme*. London: Racial Equality Unit.

US Committee for Refugees (1996) *World Refugee Survey*. Washington, DC: US Committee for Refugees.

Vygotsky, L. (1978) *Mind in Society*. Cambridge, MA: Harvard University Press.

Woodward, Will (2003) 'Culture of Tests "Stifling" Joy of Learning', *The Guardian*, 17 April.

Index